WINE HIKING OREGON

EXPLORE THE LANDSCAPES OF OREGON WINES

Wine Hiking Oregon
Explore the Landscapes of Oregon Wines
By: Jack Costa

ISBN: 9783907293966
Published by Helvetiq, Lausanne/Basel, Switzerland
Cover Design: Ajša Zdravković
Graphic Design and illustration: Daniel Malak, Jędrzej Malak (maps)
Printed in China
First Edition: May 2023

info@helvetiq.ch

www.helvetiq.com
www.facebook.com/helvetiq
instagram: @helvetiq

HEL·· VETiQ helvetiq.com

WINE HIKING OREGON

EXPLORE THE LANDSCAPES OF OREGON WINES

TABLE OF CONTENTS

1

INTRODUCTION

ABOUT THE AUTHOR

Jack Costa is a writer, podcaster, content creator, and Oregon outdoors enthusiast. After living in Sonoma County wine country for seven years, Jack moved with his family to Oregon's Umpqua Valley, a region known not only for its wines but also for its world-renowned fly-fishing and hiking. It was here in the Umpqua, the birthplace of the Oregon Pinot Noir, that Jack's journey towards writing an Oregon "wiking" book began. At seventeen, he started studying winemaking and viticulture under Stephen Reustle at Reustle Prayer Rock Vineyards. Jack spent many evenings with his winemaking mentor and his team as they tasted vino and discussed everything there was to know about wine. And while Jack was not old enough to drink, Stephen allowed him to sniff priceless bottles of wine from around the world. Years later, when he was finally able to sip the wine as well, his nose was already well trained.

Jack's love of writing eventually blended with his passion for wine when, on a whim, he applied for a writing job at the critically acclaimed media website *Wine Folly*. Much to his surprise, he got the job, gaining numerous opportunities to participate in wine-judging competitions and write for wine magazines, including that of America's largest wine education organization: The American Wine Society. While in college, Jack further developed his tasting and hiking skills in Washington State and began working at Col Solare, a winery project run by Italy's second oldest winemaking family. After college, Jack returned to the Umpqua as a wine judge and full-time writer. Living in close proximity to Crater Lake, Multnomah Falls, Silver Falls, Toketee Falls (and countless other spectacular hiking regions), it was almost inevitable that Jack would come to write a book "pairing" Oregon's best outdoor adventures with some of its best wines.

Jack still lives in the Umpqua, where you'll find him either in a wine cellar, hunting in the backwoods, or around a campfire sipping vino. You can listen to him on the *Wine Heretics* podcast and stay up to date on his activities through his website, wineheretics.com.

ABOUT WINE HIKING IN OREGON

People typically think of Oregon as a state of dense greenery, thickly forested mountains, and everlasting rain. However, there's much more to Oregon than that. The diversity of Oregon—in its geography, its geology, and its wines—cannot be overstated.

While Oregon's wine country is small in comparison to that of Washington or California, say, it is precisely this smallness that makes it great. A majority of Oregon wineries, unlike those in neighboring states, are small family-owned operations devoted to high-quality and small-lot production. The landscape surrounding this wine country ranges from picturesque rolling grasslands and meadows full of vibrant wildflowers to dramatic crags and ravines, towering mountain peaks, and majestic waterfalls. And whether the wines be warm, oaky and more delicate, or savory; fresh reds, or creamy whites with minerality and zest; the tasting options in Oregon never cease to surprise. This is due to the same regional climatic diversity that characterizes the state's diverse hiking opportunities.

The Umpqua and Willamette, the birthplaces of Oregon's wine industry, are shielded from the battering winds of the Pacific. This not only aids in maintaining a moderate climate but also makes for wonderful hiking and an abundance of breathtaking panoramic views. And while Oregon may be young as a state, it boasts no shortage of historical landmarks, antique shops, forest lodges, historic farms, pioneering trails, Native American heritage sites, and ancient lava formations. In the southernmost region of Oregon, you'll find both wine gems and 19th-century gold-mining towns. In Ashland, you'll have access to numerous world-class wines just minutes away from charming cafés, mountain hiking, and the Oregon Shakespeare Festival, one of the largest regional repertory theaters in the United States. In the northern regions of Oregon, you'll find the Gorge with the Historic Columbia River Highway and magnificent waterfall hikes.

Home to 90 of the states 250+ waterfalls, the Columbia River Gorge is rightly dubbed the waterfall mecca of Oregon. Hood River wine country rests in the heart of this mecca, a perfect spot for those seeking hiking adventures in forests, canyons, and ravines followed by world-class wine tasting experiences.

Oregon's rich volcanic past greatly influences the present, lending unique qualities to both the hikes and the wines. Advanced and novice hikers will find an abundance of thrilling outdoor experiences throughout Central Oregon. Whether you're descending into lava caves, viewing roaring waterfalls, or ascending the rugged summits of extinct volcanos, there's both a hike and a wine for just about everyone here. This region is home to the famed Smith Rock, one of the state's most visited natural spectacles.

And yes, this book is about wine, but it wouldn't do justice to Oregon without an honorable mention of its beer. Bend (and Portland) flex their beer muscles with the best of 'em. So, while you may be thirsty for some vino after a hike, be aware that there is also a stellar selection of local craft brews on tap nearby.

CHOOSE THE WINE OR THE HIKE

NAME OF THE HIKE

REGION

LEVEL OF DIFFICULTY

MAP

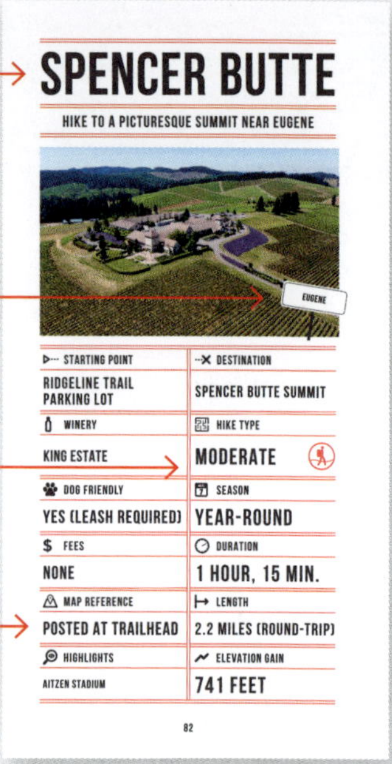

SPENCER BUTTE

HIKE TO A PICTURESQUE SUMMIT NEAR EUGENE

STARTING POINT	DESTINATION
RIDGELINE TRAIL PARKING LOT	SPENCER BUTTE SUMMIT
WINERY	HIKE TYPE
KING ESTATE	MODERATE
DOG FRIENDLY	SEASON
YES (LEASH REQUIRED)	YEAR-ROUND
FEES	DURATION
NONE	1 HOUR, 15 MIN.
MAP REFERENCE	LENGTH
POSTED AT TRAILHEAD	2.2 MILES (ROUND-TRIP)
HIGHLIGHTS	ELEVATION GAIN
AITZEN STADIUM	741 FEET

82

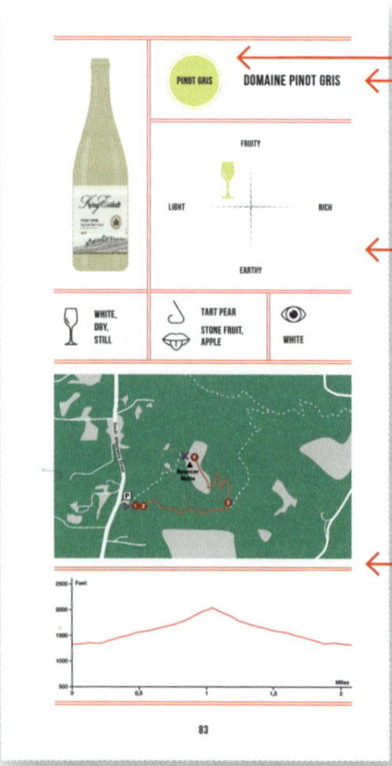

NAME OF THE GRAPE(S)

NAME OF THE WINE

INFORMATION ABOUT THE WINE

INFORMATION ABOUT THE HIKE

ON THE HIKES AND HIKE RATINGS

Each of the hikes in this book gets a difficulty rating based on several factors. While the overall length and duration of the hike is considered, the predominant differentiating factor is the relative grade of each trail. One of the best aspects of hiking in Oregon is the broad range of the physical demands placed on the hiker.

EASY

These hikes range from one to two miles, with elevation gains of 500 feet or less. Typically, they take no more than two hours to complete.

MODERATE

Moderate hikes will be three to five miles in length, feature elevation gains between 500 and 1,000 feet, and take between three and five hours to complete. A majority of the hikes in this book are rated moderate.

STRENUOUS

Strenuous hikes exceed six miles in length and have elevation gains of between 1,500 and 2,500 feet. These hikes will take five or more hours to complete and lead through some challenging terrain.

The technical data for each hike was gathered using a variety of methods, including a standard hiking and GPS app. The exact length and elevation gain were recorded during the hike and compared to the average provided by an online hiking community for the same route.

Most of the hikes are on round-trip routes on which you return from your destination the same way you arrived there, but there are a number of trails consisting of loops.

Most of the featured trails require some form of usage-fee permit. This can usually be purchased online ahead of time, but you can often pay cash for a standard day-use fee at the trailhead. Some parks require additional permits, depending on the area and the season. Be sure to look up the required passes or fees before going on each hike. The fees won't exceed a few dollars, so rest assured you won't be breaking the bank to go hiking.

Be sure to download additional maps and essential information about each trail prior to setting off. If you want to bring your dog along, be sure to check the trail website or contact the land manager before setting off. Where dogs are allowed, they generally must be kept on leash. I also recommend that you contact the wineries before visiting. Hours of operation can vary considerably depending on the season and location.

ON THE WINERIES AND WINE RATINGS

It may come as no surprise that Oregon's reputation rests primarily on the Pinot Noir grape. Many people fail to realize, however, that there's more on offer in the Beaver State than this delicate Burgundian red grape. In Southern Oregon, you'll find a plethora of wines that contradict Oregon's "cool climate" stereotype. The Rouge, Applegate, and Bear Creek viticultural areas feature the heat-loving Cabernet Sauvignon, Syrah, Malbec, and an abundance of white wines. In the Umpqua, you'll not only find Oregon's oldest producer of Pinot Noir but also Tempranillo and Albarino reminiscent of Spain, Gruner Veltliner akin to that in Austria, and Rieslings rivaling those of Alsace. As you travel north, the Willamette Valley, though the prince of Pinot Noir, offers an exciting selection of Pinot Gris, Sauvignon Blanc, and crisp Chardonnay crafted in the more feminine Burgundian style. The Columbia River Gorge is home to several wine and hiking gems not found anywhere else in the state. Juicy robust reds like Zinfandel, Cabernet Sauvignon, and Merlot abound, with some limited plantings of Grenache and even the Italian grape Barbera. In Bend you'll find tasting-room transplants from Walla Walla and some wineries devoted to crafting interesting and high-quality cold-hardy grapes. And let's not forget about Oregon's Rocks District in Walla Walla, which has consistently excelled at making some of the world's most distinctive Syrah.

The wines I chose to feature are typically the winery's flagship variety or blend. Most of the wines are available year-round. Because Oregon is Pinot Noir–centric, you'll find several distinct expressions of this grape. Yet I purposefully chose from a wide variety of grapes and wine styles in order to highlight the many different qualities of Oregon wine. In addition, I attempted (aside from Pinot Noir) not to cover particular grape varieties more than once. The wines, just like the wineries, were chosen based on a high volume of superb consumer reviews and numerous accolades from highly regarded international wine competitions and publications. The tasting notes are subjective and represent my own particular spin on the qualities of each of the wines.

Reservation requirements can vary, so it's always best to call and inquire before visiting the wineries. Many wineries offer food as well as wine, but often not a full post-hike meal. Rather, they tend to offer creamy cheeses, specialty hors d'oeuvres, and hardy meats that function primarily as wine pairings. Not to worry, however—many of the hikes end in close proximity to delicious eateries, restaurants, food trucks, and, dare I say it, good breweries.

Remember, wine hiking is fun, but it's important to drink responsibly and stay safe. Eat food before tasting and make sure you're well hydrated. If you feel even slightly buzzed, do not drive. Plan to have a designated driver. Safety is your top priority.

PREPARING FOR YOUR HIKE

Whether on a 1–2-hour trek or a 6–10-mile all-day hike, you'll want to carry certain essentials to ensure a safe and enjoyable hiking experience. A little carelessness goes a long way, but so can a little common sense and wisdom. No matter how experienced you are, you never know when a little practical knowledge could save you from a very unpleasant afternoon and/or trip to the ER. And though you can't avoid some things, you can at least prepare as best as you possibly can. Wine hiking is supposed to be fun, not dangerous. Always bring along a small backpack to carry your belongings. It doesn't have to be fancy, but should suffice to carry the items listed below.

MAPS AND NAVIGATION

The small overview maps provided in this book are not meant to be used in place of an actual map of the hiking area. Be sure to have an actual map (digital or print) and additional navigational tools when hiking. It may seem silly to some, but having a compass on hand is never a bad thing. Some hiking aficionados might prefer the tried-and-true compass given to them by their great-grandfather. There are, however, digital compasses available that you can easily download as an app. Since many of these hikes have little to no cell service, do be sure to download all maps and directions before you set off.

LIGHT

If you unexpectedly find yourself in some remote and dreary wilderness, bound for calamity in complete and utter despair, a light will at least make the experience more visual. A headlamp or small flashlight will serve you well when hiking anywhere in the world. It's always good to have an extra set of batteries or a power bank with you, too.

HYDRATION

No matter how short the hike, never fail to bring water. While Oregon may generally have a mild climate, don't underestimate your need for H_2O. Backpacks with water bladders are convenient, and many hold several quarts of water. If possible, invest in a high-quality water filter or UV-light water purifier. During one of the more strenuous hikes in this book, I ran out of water. Thankfully, my handy water filter worked its magic on fresh waterfall water to refill my bottle. I always recommend having extra water available in your car for after a hike. Remember: Staying hydrated is especially important if you're tasting wine!

NUTRITION

Be sure to bring extra snacks and high-calorie protein bars or trail mix. You want have plenty of fuel for the trail. Packing dried meats—like beef or chicken jerky—sandwiches, or even fruit is great for maintaining your blood sugar levels. As with water, bring more than you need. Hiking is a calorie burner, and you don't want to have a food crash on the trail. Keeping an extra stash of nonperishable food in your car can be helpful in the event you find yourself absolutely famished after a hike.

GEAR

Hiking shoes are the number-one priority. Quality footwear makes all the difference and can make the hiking experience so much better, or so much worse! Durable clothing and a small backpack (for your water and medical supplies) are also essential. Be sure to carry or wear a fleece and a waterproof shell for protection against the elements. A sun hat and a warm hat are equally important; the former protects against sunstroke, the latter against heat loss (which occurs disproportionately through the head). Be sure to apply sunscreen even if it's overcast (you can still easily burn). Sunburn can damage your skin and cause dehydration. Carrying a knife, even a small one, can make all the difference. You never know when you'll need it. A knife and a roll of duct tape have a wide range of outdoor applications! And remember, it's better to be overly prepared than not at all.

WEATHER

Oregon has fairly predictable weather patterns, so you'll rarely be caught off guard. However, there are always exceptions. The Columbia Gorge is known for its tumultuous winds; Willamette Valley is cool and wet in the winter; the Umpqua Valley is fairly mild year-round, with a light dusting of snow every other year that melts before noon. The Siskiyou mountains in the south have more unpredictable weather patterns, as does the Oregon Coast Range. For accurate forecasts, check with the National Weather Service at www.weather.gov.

FIRE STARTER

You probably won't need a reliable lighter or fire-starting device on these hikes, but if you do find yourself stranded somewhere, a lighter could make a world of difference. Because lighters are inexpensive, I carry several in case one fails to function properly. Follow all applicable fire-safety rules, especially in the summer. Oregon and the Pacific Northwest have become increasingly known for their wildfires.

FIRST AID

Whether you're high in a rugged mountain range or meandering along an urban trail, never go without first-aid supplies. Band-Aids, bandages, ibuprofen, antiseptic and sanitation wipes, cotton swabs, and tweezers should always be on hand. If possible, carry a first-aid instructional booklet and read up beforehand, especially if you're unfamiliar with first-aid practices. Even mild injuries can become serious if not properly attended to.

SHELTER

Having a temporary shelter is important if you should get injured and the weather turn bad. This might be a simple tarp, a poncho, or a space blanket.

SANITATION

When mother nature calls, you answer. And often, she'll call unexpectedly while you're hiking. If she does, bury any #2 "disposables" roughly a foot underground, away from the trail and at least 60 yards from streams, rivers, or lakes. It's always best to bring a supply of TP and a bottle of extra hand sanitizer or wipes.

HUNTING SEASON

Generally speaking, hikers won't have to worry about hunting season in Oregon. While there is a dedicated hunting population here in the Beaver State, most of the hikes featured in this book are on land where all forms of hunting are prohibited. If you happen to visit a winery and suddenly hear loud cracking sounds rippling through the air, rest assured—it's not hunters firing their rifles but bird cannons. These are fired to scare birds away from the vineyards and ensure they don't eat the precious fruit.

DRONES

In recent years, drone photography has become a popular pastime, particularly among outdoor enthusiasts and hikers. Drone legislation is constantly in flux, and staying abreast of up-to-date information can be difficult. If you are one of the many emerging drone hobbyists who wish to be responsible pilots, there are a few things to consider when hiking in Oregon. Sometimes the land manager and website will indicate whether the use of drones is prohibited. Sometimes, it just isn't clear. The best way to obtain information is to call the land manager and ask a ranger. In fact, asking a ranger for permission to fly your drone (and especially to take drone photographs), even though you may not be required to ask, will always be appreciated.

ADDITIONAL RESOURCES

SOUTHERN OREGON

Hiking: www.travelmedford.org,
Wineries: www.southernoregon.org
Visitor Amenities: www.recreation.gov, jacksoncountyor.org

WILLAMETTE VALLEY & THE COAST

Hiking: www.alltrails.com, www.oregonhikers.org
Wineries: www.willamettevalley.org, oregonwine.org
Visitor Amenities: www.recreation.gov, www.fs.usda.gov/willamette

COLUMBIA GORGE & EASTERN OREGON

Hiking: gorgefriends.org
Wineries: www.gorgewine.com, oregonwine.org
Visitor Amenities: visitcolumbiarivergorge.com

CENTRAL OREGON

Hiking: oregonhikers.org, alltrails.com
Wineries: www.eatdrinkbend.com, wallawallavalleywine.com
Visitor Amenities: www.visitbend.com, wallawalla.org

TRAIL ETIQUETTE

With literally thousands of trails, it's no surprise that Oregon has become one of the top hiking destinations in the United States. Many new trails are under development, and old ones are being expanded or repaired. Many of these fabulous trails are heavily used and are suffering from increased wear and tear. As hikers, we have a certain responsibility toward helping maintain and preserve these wonderful trails, not just for ourselves but also for the enjoyment of others. It is therefore important to know the various spoken (and unspoken) rules of hiking.

STAY ON THE TRAIL

This sounds simple, but many people deviate from the indicated path. As respectful hikers, we ought to conserve not just the trail, but also the surrounding natural beauty. We are here to appreciate and observe Mother Nature, not to disrupt her. Deviating from the trail also increases your risk of stumbling upon forms of wildlife you might not wish to encounter. This includes various bugs! Always check for ticks after a hike. These bloodsucking critters are known for finding their way onto you or your dog while hiking.

DON'T INTERACT WITH WILDLIFE

Unless necessary, leave wildlife alone. As a hiker, you'll undoubtedly encounter some furry creatures here and there. Don't feed them and don't disturb them. This goes for plants as well. Don't modify or remove the plant growth, especially if you don't know what the plant is. Yes, it may look pretty, but it might just be poison oak, the oils of which cause a puffy red rash with incessant itchiness and irritation.

NOISE

Enjoy the solitude of nature. Don't be overly noisy. Don't bring a stereo system with you. (Believe me, I've seen it several times). Not only is this disrespectful of other hikers but it disturbs wildlife and the overall ambiance of your own hike. Wearing headphones might not disturb other hikers, but it will impede your abilities to listen to your surroundings. Just because you can't see danger doesn't mean it's not there. Use your ears.

PICK UP YOUR TRASH

Don't litter, and if you do see trash, dispose of it in the appropriate manner. Even if your trash is biodegradable, pick it up. Keep the trail clean and **Leave No Trace**. Carry a small plastic bag for waste or scraps.

BE FRIENDLY

You will undoubtedly encounter other hikers during your wine hiking. Greet them with a smile on your face and yield to hikers who might be trying to pass. Treat others on the trail as you would want to be treated yourself.

2

MAP & INDEX

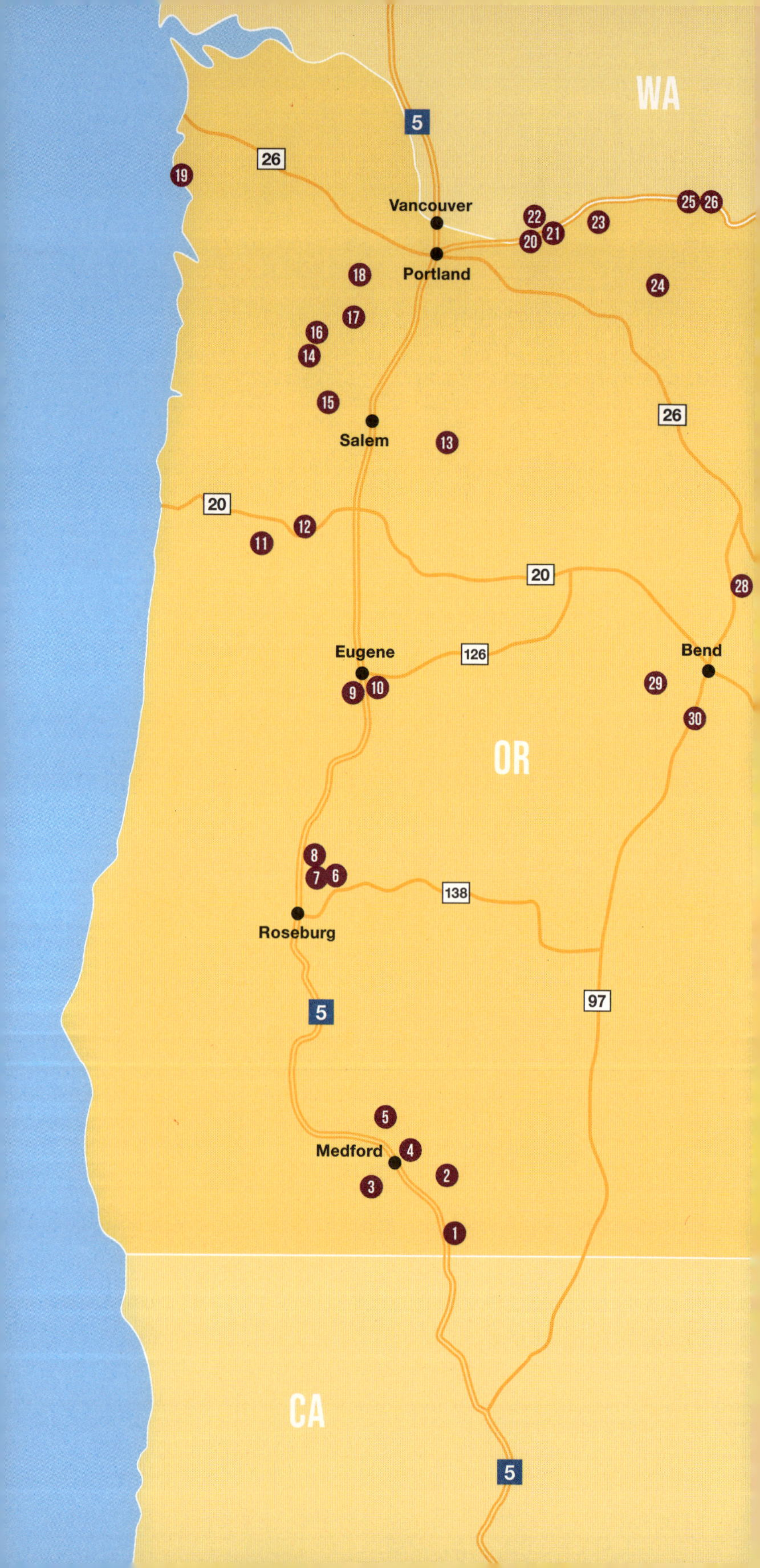
WA
OR
CA
Vancouver
Portland
Salem
Eugene
Roseburg
Medford
Bend
5
26
20
126
138
97
1
2
3
4
5
6
7
8
9
10
11
12
13
14
15
16
17
18
19
20
21
22
23
24
25
26
28
29
30

MAP

HIKES

NAME OF THE ROUTE	TOWN, STATE	LENGTH	PAGE
Angel's Rest	Corbett	4.8 Miles (Round-Trip)	140
Bald Hill	Corvallis	3.4 Miles (Round-Trip)	94
Cape Falcon	Nahalem	4.2 Miles	132
Chehalem Ridge	Gaston	6.3 Miles (Round-Trip)	126
Cooper Creek Reservoir	Sutherlin	5.5 Miles (Loop)	72
East Applegate Ridge	Jacksonville	4.6 Miles (Round-Trip)	42
Misery Ridge and Summit Trail	Bend	6 Miles (Loop)	188
Grizzly Peak	Ashland	4.8 Miles (Loop)	38
Lava River Cave Hike	Bend	2.2 Miles (Round-Trip)	200
Left Coast Cellars	Salem	1 Mile (Loop)	110
Lower Table Rock Trail	Central Point	5.8 Miles (Round-Trip)	54
Marys Peak Summit Hike	Philomath	5.2 Miles (Round-Trip)	90
Miller Woods	Mcminnville	4.1 Miles (Loop)	116
Mount Pisgah Summit Trail	Eugene	3.4 Miles (Round-Trip)	86
Multnomah Falls	Portland	2.4 Miles (Round-Trip)	144
North Bank Habitat (Comstock)	Roseburg	5.4 Miles (Loop)	60
North Bank Habitat Management Area	Roseburg	5.9 Miles (Loop)	66
Pilot Rock	Ashland	2.8 Miles (Round-Trip)	32
Punch Bowl Falls	Columbia Gorge	4.0 Miles (Round-Trip)	156
Roxy Ann Peak Trail	Medford	5 Miles (Round-Trip)	48
Silver Falls Canyon Trail Loop	Salem	5.6 Miles (Loop)	100
South Fork Walla Walla	Milton-	4.2 Miles (Round-Trip)	180
Spencer Butte	Eugene	2.2 Miles (Round-Trip)	80
Tamanawas Falls	Mount Hood	3.4 Miles (Round-Trip)	162
Tom Mccall Point Trail	Mosier	4.5 Miles (Round-Trip)	174
Trappist Abbey Guadalupe Loop	Lafayette	4 Miles (Loop)	120
Tumalo Falls	Bend	6.4 Miles (Round-Trip)	194
Twin Tunnels	Mosier	3.7 Miles (Round-Trip)	168
Wahkeena Falls	Corbett	2 Miles (Round-Trip)	150
Yamhill Valley Vineyards	Mcminnville	2.4 Miles (Loop)	106

WINERIES & WINES

3

THE WINE HIKES

SOUTHERN OREGON

PILOT ROCK

A TOWERING VOLCANIC NECK IN THE CASCADE SISKIYOU WILDERNESS

STARTING POINT	DESTINATION
PILOT ROCK TRAILHEAD	PILOT ROCK
WINERY	**HIKE TYPE**
WEISINGER FAMILY WINERY	MODERATE
DOG FRIENDLY	**SEASON**
YES (LEASH REQUIRED)	YEAR-ROUND
FEES	**DURATION**
NONE	2 HOURS
MAP REFERENCE	**LENGTH**
POSTED AT TRAILHEAD	2.8 MILES (ROUND-TRIP)
HIGHLIGHTS	**ELEVATION GAIN**
PACIFIC CREST TRAIL, MOUNT SHASTA	810 FEET

TEMPRANILLO

ESTATE TEMPRANILLO

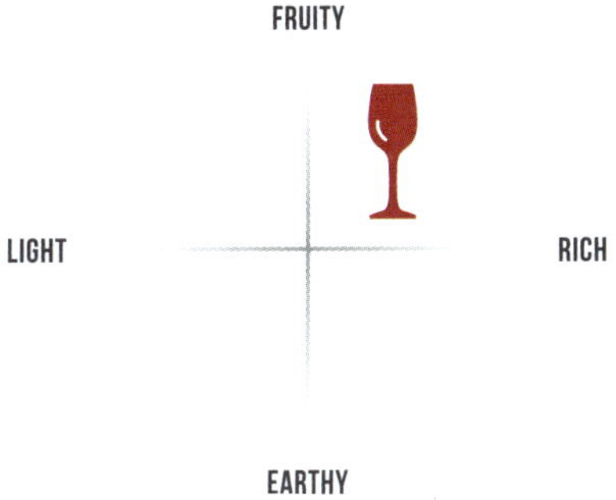

RED,
DRY,
STILL

DARK CHERRIES,
SMOKE,
SPICE,
VANILLA

DARK RUBY

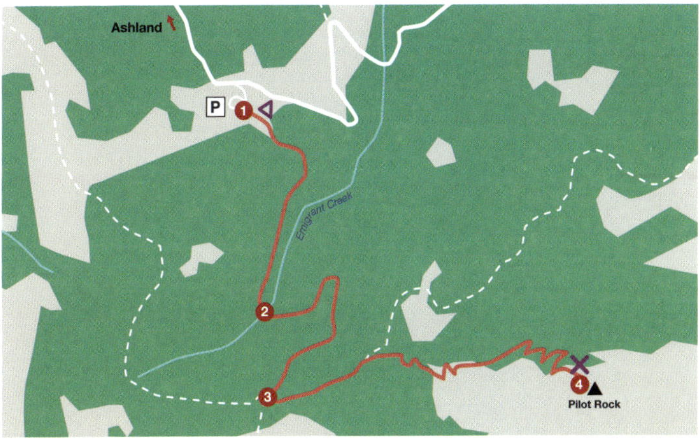

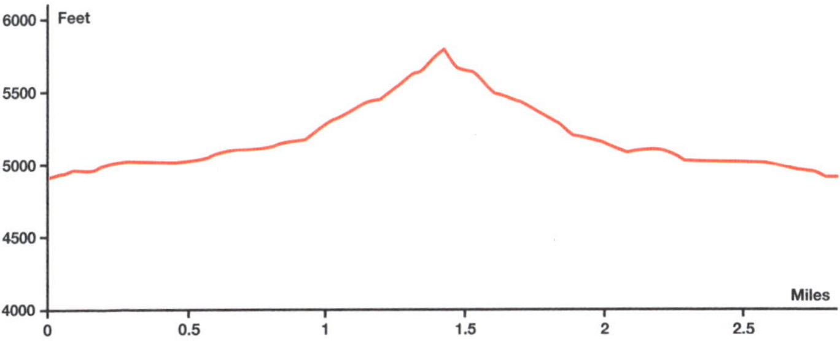

HIKE DESCRIPTION

Hike back in time to an ancient rock formation that served as a hideout for the perpetrators of the last great train robbery. Then go full steam ahead to wine tasting at one of southern Oregon's most reputable wineries.

Pilot Rock, with its breathtaking views of the Siskiyou Mountains, was once the location of several dramatic events that wouldn't be out of place in an Agatha Christie novel or Hitchcock film. The three DeAutremont brothers are said to have camped near Pilot Rock after a failed train robbery. A nationwide manhunt came to an end thanks to the efforts of the "American Sherlock," Edward Heinrich. The 1920s tale is a dramatic story to "pair" with a Pilot Rock hike. Modern day hikers can enjoy the same views as early settlers, who used the spiral, columnar-shaped basalt tower as a lookout when traveling from California to Oregon. The panoramic views of Mount Shasta, Mount McLoughlin, and the Trinity Alps Wilderness of Northern California are not to be missed.

A little less than half a mile down the trail, you'll cross Emigrant Creek, a tributary that feeds the larger Bear Creek of Jacksonville County. In just over half a mile, you'll cross the fork of the Pilot Rock Trail and the Pacific Crest Trail. For the last mile, the trail ascends in a series of steep but rocky switchbacks that conclude at the base of Pilot Rock. The trail ends here, but more adventurous individuals might attempt the rigorous climb to the top of Pilot Rock. Although not incredibly difficult, you should be cautious: refrain from climbing if the rock is wet or damp. If you do the climb and reach the top, you'll be looking out at the same jagged peaks and mountain ridges as the pioneers who visited Pilot Rock so many generations ago. For those interested, there is a trail to Pilot Rock from the Pacific Crest Trail, but this adds an additional 4 miles to the hike.

TURN-BY-TURN DIRECTIONS

1. From the Pilot Rock trailhead, proceed through the forest towards Emigrant Creek.
2. At 0.3 miles, cross Emigrant Creek.
3. At 0.7 miles, cross the junction of the Pilot Rock Trail and turn left onto the Pacific Crest Trail. (Path becomes Pilot Rock Trail again after 0.2 miles.)
4. At 1.4 miles, reach the end of the Pilot Rock Trail. Return the way you came.

FIND THE TRAILHEAD

From Ashland, head south onto I-5. Travel for 6.4 miles and take Exit 6 onto Old Highway 99. Continue for 4.0 miles before turning left onto 40-2E-33. Drive for 0.7 miles to the Pilot Rock Trailhead.

WEISINGER FAMILY WINERY

With winemaking dreams larger than the state of Texas, John Weisinger relocated from the Lone Star State to Ashland, Oregon in the early 1970s. There he established a vineyard and winemaking operation. John's son Eric has since inherited the title of winemaker, leading the Weisinger team to critical acclaim for their Chardonnay, Malbec, Greneche, Pinot Noir, and Tempranillo. Spicy, smoky, and laced with firm tannins, the Weisinger Tempranillo will excite both novice and expert wine drinkers. This wine segues the classic elements of the beloved Spanish wine into a New World style. Eric spent time in New Zealand, California, and Oregon and gained an intricate understanding of crafting premium wine...and the proof is in the pudding (or, rather, the wine). Join the hospitable Weisinger staff for an elevated tasting experience of delicious world-class wine, imbued with the spirit of Southern Oregon.

Tempranillo: It wasn't until the early 1990s that Tempranillo began to develop an international reputation. Once only recognized in Spain, it began to be promoted more widely by producers like Spain's Vega Sicilia and Abacela in Oregon, and finally caught the attention of the mainstream wine world. Most of Rioja's wine growing is devoted to Tempranillo, which produces good quality wines for affordable prices. Tempranillo wines generally have a more densely structured personality than those made from other grapes. This is mostly due to their high tannin concentration, which also helps to extend Tempranillo's longevity and aging potential. (Many great vintages can age 50+ years, with some rare bottlings reaching upward of 100 years.) With such pronounced tannins and an affinity for oak, Tempranillo is typically aged in barrels, which helps to soften the mouthfeel and contributes smoky, chocolatey, and spicy characteristics to the final product.

LAND MANAGER

BLM Medford District Office
3040 Biddle Road
Medford, OR 97504
Phone: (541) 618-2200
www.blm.gov

WINERY

Weisinger Family Winery
3150 Siskiyou Blvd
Ashland, OR 97520
Phone: (541) 488-5989
www.weisingers.com
Distance from trailhead: 11.7 miles

GRIZZLY PEAK

ASCEND GRIZZLY PEAK FOR A VIEW OF THE SISKIYOUS

STARTING POINT	DESTINATION
GRIZZLY PEAK TRAILHEAD	GRIZZLY PEAK SUMMIT
WINERY	HIKE TYPE
IRVINE AND ROBERTS ESTATE	MODERATE
DOG FRIENDLY	SEASON
YES (LEASH REQUIRED)	YEAR-ROUND
FEES	DURATION
NONE	2 HOURS
MAP REFERENCE	LENGTH
POSTED AT TRAILHEAD	4.8 MILES (LOOP)
HIGHLIGHTS	ELEVATION GAIN
OREGON SHAKESPEARE THEATERS	921 FEET

CHARDONNAY

ESTATE CHARDONNAY

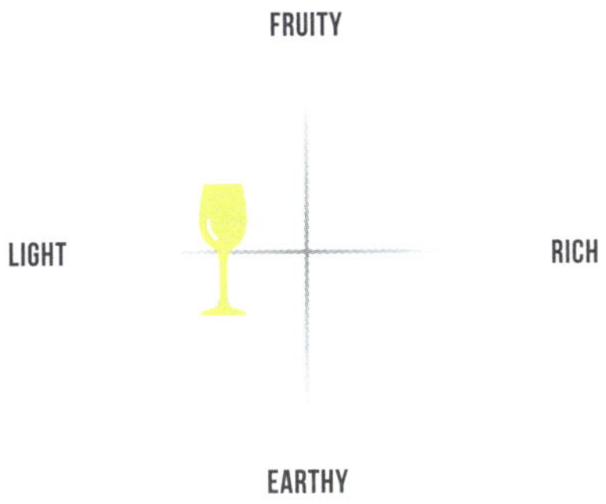

WHITE,
DRY,
STILL

APPLE,
PEAR,
PEACH,
ZIPPY ACIDITY

STRAW

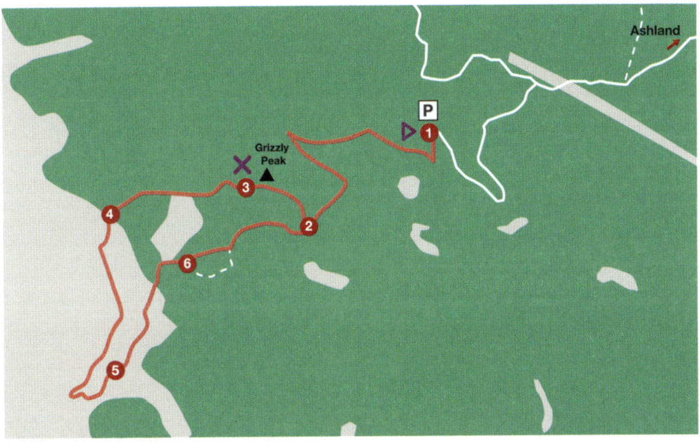

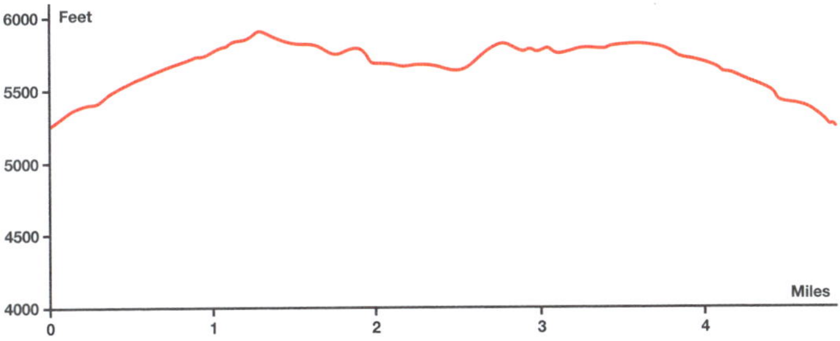

HIKE DESCRIPTION

Climb up to a panoramic view of Southern Oregon's Grizzly peak and then enjoy a tasting in Ashland, home of the Oregon Shakespeare Festival.

Legend says this hike is named "Grizzly Peak" because of its proximity to the site of the last grizzly-bear sighting in Southern Oregon in 1890. Located northeast of Ashland, the trail offers hikers sweeping views of the Siskiyou Mountains, the Three Sisters, Mount McLoughlin, and the Ashland Valley. Once on the trail, you'll notice the terrain quickly changing. The valley's rolling hills straddled with oaks will disappear as you begin your ascent. The trail begins with switchbacks that wind through a forest before emerging into meadows peppered with wildflowers that bloom throughout June and July. After about a mile, look for a sign at the fork and turn right to proceed past the summit. The summit is basically just a pile of earth and rocks, but the best views are yet to come. The path will eventually veer out of the forest and toward an open ridge running along the western side of the mountain. In 2002, a wildfire cleared some of the forest, which means you'll have unimpeded views of dramatic mountain ridges. The path climbs toward several more lookouts—each more spectacular than the last. When you reach the final outlook at 3.1 miles, the stunning views of Southern Oregon will make you feel like you're on top of the world.

TURN-BY-TURN DIRECTIONS

1. From the Grizzly Peak Trailhead, proceed 1.1 miles through the forest.
2. At 1.1 miles, turn right at the fork and follow the sign for the Loop Trail.
3. At 1.4 miles, reach the summit (marked by a pile of boulders).
4. At 2.1 miles, reach the outlook and the site of the 2002 fire.
5. At 2.9 miles, reach the next series of outlooks and take in the panoramic views.
6. At 3.1 miles, arrive at the final outlook. Continue on the trail for 1.6 miles back to the trailhead.

FIND THE TRAILHEAD

From I-5 South toward Ashland, take Exit 14 and proceed east on Highway 66. Travel for 0.25 miles and turn left onto Dead Indian Memorial Road. Continue for 6.7 miles. Turn left at Shale City Road (#38-2E-27). Continue for 3.0 miles and then turn left at #38-2E-9.2. Proceed for 2.0 miles to arrive at the trailhead.

IRVINE AND ROBERTS

What do wine and Shakespeare have in common? Ashland, Oregon. A haven for drama and all things artsy, Ashland attracts thousands of visitors each year with its wine, outdoor activities, and annual Shakespeare festival. Five miles from downtown Ashland, Irvine and Roberts focuses its production almost exclusively on Pinot Noir and Chardonnay, though it also makes smaller volumes of Pinot Meunier. The 80-acre family ranch sits at 2,000 feet in the gentle rolling hills at the base of the Cascade and Siskiyou Mountain ranges. This unique climate is ideal for crafting cooler-climate Burgundian wine varieties. Zippy, polished, and nothing short of refreshing, the Irvine and Roberts estate Chardonnay will quench your thirst after a hike to the top of Grizzly Peak. The patio offers panoramic views of the Cascades that you can enjoy while pairing your wine with an artisan charcuterie platter assembled from locally made cheeses, crispy crackers, olives, and other bite-sized appetizers.

Chardonnay: The chief white wine grape of Burgundy, Chardonnay has established a firm reputation in Oregon for creating clean and refreshing wines that contrast the more heavily oaked and buttery examples found in California.

LAND MANAGER

BLM Medford District Office
3040 Biddle Road
Medford, OR 97504
Phone: (541) 618-2200
www.blm.gov

WINERY

Irvine and Roberts
1614 Emigrant Creek Rd
Ashland, OR 97520
Phone: (541) 482-9383
irvinerobertsvineyards.com
Distance from trailhead: 12.4 miles

EAST APPLEGATE RIDGE

A RIDGE WALK WITH STUNNING VIEWS OF THE APPLEGATE VALLEY

STARTING POINT	DESTINATION
STERLING CREEK ROAD TRAILHEAD	APPLEGATE VALLEY LOOKOUT BENCH
WINERY	HIKE TYPE
DANCIN	MODERATE
DOG FRIENDLY	SEASON
YES (LEASH REQUIRED)	YEAR-ROUND
FEES	DURATION
NONE	2 HOURS 20 MIN.
MAP REFERENCE	LENGTH
POSTED AT TRAILHEAD	4.6 MILES (ROUND-TRIP)
HIGHLIGHTS	ELEVATION GAIN
HISTORIC DOWNTOWN JACKSONVILLE	298 FEET

PINOT NOIR

SETTI PEZZI PINOT NOIR

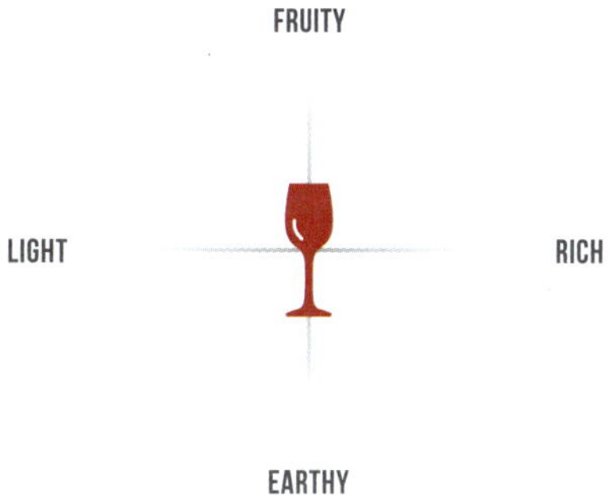

RED,
DRY,
STILL

LIGHT CHERRIES,
RED FRUIT,
VANILLA,
SPICE

RUBY

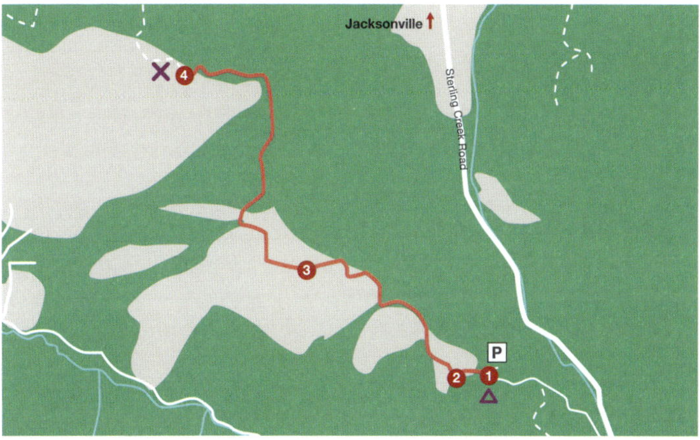

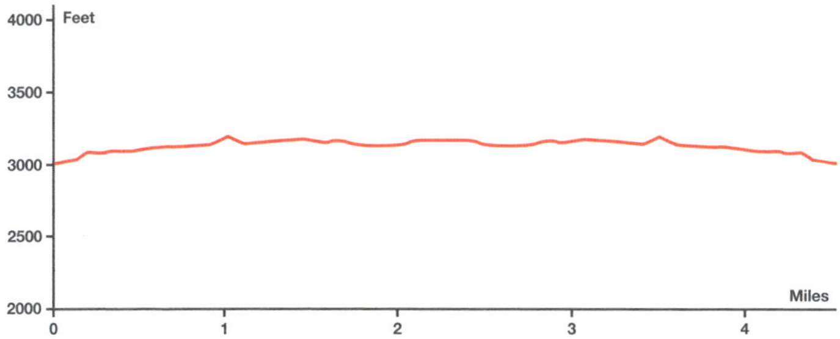

HIKE DESCRIPTION

Enjoy dramatic views of the Applegate Valley and the Cascades and then dance on over for a treat at one of Jacksonville's finest tasting rooms and wineries.

Opened in 2017, the East Applegate Ridge Trail is the result of the collaborative efforts of the Bureau of Land Management and the Applegate Trails Association. Stretching roughly 5 miles from point to point (10 miles to the end and back), this trail's claim to fame is its dramatic views of the Cascade Mountain Range. The first half of the hike is the more spectacular, so I recommend turning back after reaching the wooden rest bench at 2.3 miles—but not before snapping some panoramic photos! On a nice day, you might even spy dozens of paragliders soaring above the Cascades.

From the trailhead, the first two miles will take you along an open ridgeline that offers expansive views of the Applegate valley, which is dotted with small farms and vineyards. In the distance, you'll see thickly forested peaks brushing the bellies of the clouds. The valley is named after one of Oregon's most influential pioneering families, the Applegates. With tension growing between the settlers and the British over the Oregon territory (a remnant of the War of 1812), the Applegates established the trail to provide a safer route to Oregon.

Due to the lack of shade, I recommend you attempt this portion of the trail in the morning, before the afternoon heat sets in. Between March and May, you'll find an abundance of bright yellow, purple, and red wildflowers along the way. But be careful: poison oak is as bountiful as the wildflowers and the breathtaking views. Continue on the trail until you reach a wooden bench and a lookout area. It's best to turn back here, as the remainder of the trail passes through thick woodlands without much in the way of views.

TURN-BY-TURN DIRECTIONS

1. From Sterling Creek Road, follow the direction indicated by the small and somewhat hidden sign for the East Applegate Ridge Trail.
2. At 0.1 miles reach the first viewpoint. (Check the skies for paragliders!)
3. At 0.6 miles, reach the second outlook area and take in the views of Applegate Valley.
4. At 2.3 miles, arrive at the lookout bench. Return the way you came.

FIND THE TRAILHEAD

From Jacksonville, head south on S 4th St. towards W Main St. for 50 feet, then turn right onto West Main Street. Continue for 0.1 miles. Turn left onto S Oregon Street for 0.1 miles. Turn left onto Applegate Street and continue for 1.7 miles; then turn left onto Sterling Creek Road. Proceed on Sterling Creek Road for 4.1 miles. Then turn right onto Upper Poorman Creek Road/BLM Road 38-2-29.1. The parking lot is on the left after 0.6 miles.

DANCIN VINEYARDS

Founded in 2008 by Dan and Cindy Marca, DANCIN Vineyards (a combination of the owners' names) is located five minutes from historic downtown Jacksonville. DANCIN offers delicious bottlings of several different grapes and breathtaking views of the ancient volcanic terrain of Southern Oregon's Table Rocks, the Rouge Valley, and Mount McLoughlin. Perched on a small hillside, the DANCIN tasting room, fashioned like that of an Italian villa, overlooks the 27-acre estate vineyards, which grow mostly Pinot Noir and Chardonnay. Upon arrival, you'll ascend a winding path through a small parcel of vineyard to reach the cozy tasting room and pavilion, which are surrounded by gardens of colorful Japanese maples and an adorable koi pond. The winery crafts superb Syrah, Chardonnay, Zinfandel, Sangiovese, and even Barbera, with Pinot Noir leading the pack. Arguably as delicious as its wine is DANCIN's selection of mouthwatering hors d'oeuvres. Think mushrooms stuffed with Italian sausage and drenched with Chardonnay cream sauce; artisan pizzas; pane caldo flatbreads glazed with garlic-infused olive oil; formaggio boards with fresh fruit, housemade pickles, mustard, and crackers; and much, much more! If that description wasn't enough to make your mouth water, DANCIN also offers a port-style wine made from Barbera, which pairs harmoniously with the vineyard's homemade vanilla-bean ice cream and an espresso! Delish. Before visiting, be sure to look at the website, which often announces the date and time of live music performances. Reservations are highly recommended. And if you're still looking to explore (or eat more food), Jacksonville's main street is lined with museums, theaters, adorable cafés, great restaurants, and lively pubs.

Pinot Noir: Literally "black pine," Pinot Noir is the predominant red wine grape in Burgundy, and any wine labeled "Burgundy" is actually a Pinot Noir. Pinot Noir is characterized by delicate floral aromas and savory light berry flavors. In the past century, the grape has done incredibly well in Oregon, which has rightly been called the New World counterpart of Burgundy.

LAND MANAGER

BLM Medford District Office
3040 Biddle Road
Medford, OR 97504
Phone: (541) 618-2200
www.blm.gov

WINERY

Dancin vineyards
4477 S Stage Rd,
Medford, OR 97501
Phone: (541) 245-1133
www.dancin.com
Distance from trailhead: 7.9 miles

ROXY ANN PEAK TRAIL

HIKE TO THE SUMMIT OF A DORMANT VOLCANO

STARTING POINT	DESTINATION
MADRONE TRAILHEAD	ROXY ANN SUMMIT
WINERY	HIKE TYPE
ROXYANN WINERY	MODERATE
DOG FRIENDLY	SEASON
YES (LEASH REQUIRED)	YEAR-ROUND
FEES	DURATION
NONE	2 HOURS 30 MIN.
MAP REFERENCE	LENGTH
POSTED AT TRAILHEAD	3,2 MILES (ROUND-TRIP)
HIGHLIGHTS	ELEVATION GAIN
RIM OF CRATER LAKE	1,036 FEET

PETITE SYRAH

ESTATE PETITE SYRAH

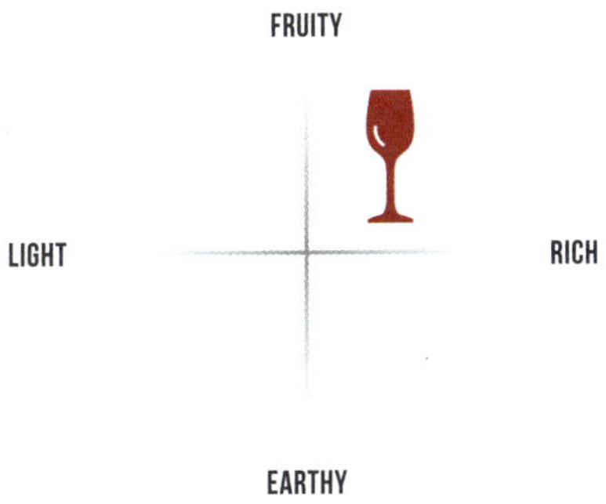

RED, DRY, STILL

DARK BLACKBERRY, CHERRY, FULL-BODIED

RED

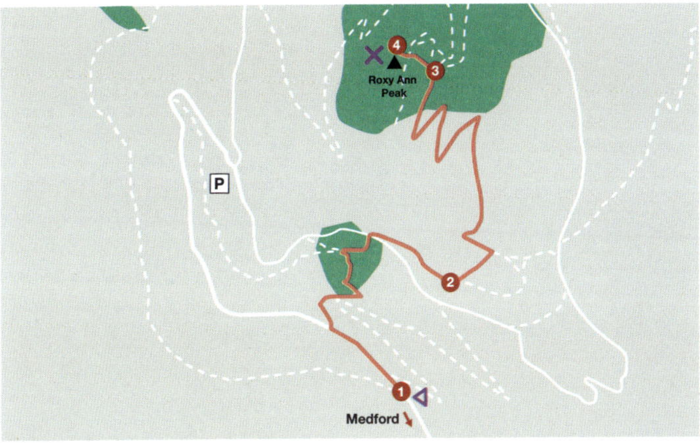

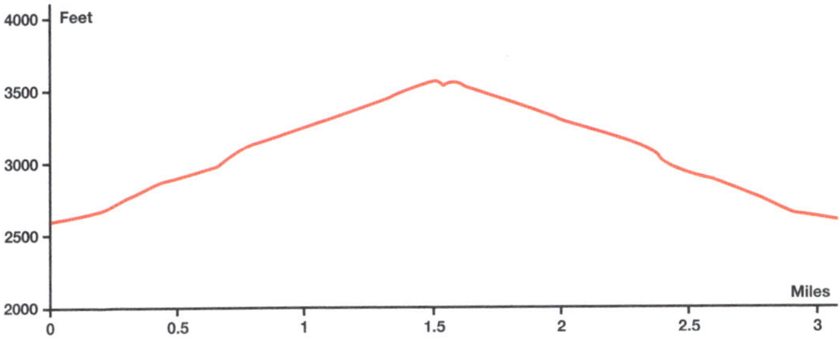

HIKE DESCRIPTION

Trek up a dormant volcano for views of nearby ancient peaks and landscapes. Afterward, learn about Oregon's pioneer history while indulging in a wine tasting at one of the oldest orchards in the state.

Roxy Ann Mountain is a delightful hike in Oregon wine country. This dormant Cascadian volcano is crisscrossed by a system of trails that give hikers views of Mount McLoughlin, Mount Thielsen, Mount Shasta, and even the rim of Crater Lake! Legend has it that Roxy Ann was used as a lookout by the Takelma tribe before the arrival of the pioneers. Dotted with picnic and rest areas, the 6-mile network of alpine trails is also horse and bike-friendly. Go early because the park gate is locked at dusk. The Madrone Trail is an enjoyable but moderate hike that begins with ascending switchbacks surrounded by oak trees. It then descends into a rich woodland area enclosed by a shaded haven of madrones. You'll stay right at an unmarked crossing to begin the Manzanita Trail, a rocky path that runs along open ridgelines with views of a sculpted volcanic landscape. The trail climbs upward in a series of switchbacks before hitting the summit, where picnic tables provide a place to rest before you head back down.

TURN-BY-TURN DIRECTIONS

1. Start at the Madrone Trailhead just above the first parking lot (past the two gates).
2. At 0.7 miles, continue right at the unmarked crossing. Cross the road and take the Manzanita Trail.
3. At 1.5 miles, the trail begins the final ascent to the Roxy Ann summit.
4. At 1.6 miles, reach the summit and its picnic tables. Return the way you came.

FIND THE TRAILHEAD

From I-5 S, take Exit 30. Turn left onto OR-62 E. At 0.5 miles, turn right on Poplar Drive and continue for 0.9 miles. Turn left onto E McAndrews Drive. Proceed for 3.8 miles to Hillcrest Road. Continue down Hillcrest Road for 1.1 miles. Turn left on Roxy Ann Road and follow it for 2.7 miles to the Prescott Park parking area.

ROXYANN WINERY

At RoxyAnn Winery, vineyards grow side by side with orchards, making for a delightful wine-tasting experience. Named after the pioneer settler RoxyAnn Bowen, the property is one of the oldest orchards in Oregon and is on the National Register of Historic Places. The RoxyAnn team planted 70 acres of wine grapes on the 200-plus acre property and produced their first vintage in 2001. Fashioned from the original "Honor Barn," the tasting room is sure to make visitors feel nostalgic. While RoxyAnn is devoted to crafting wine, the winery also carries on the family tradition of selling fresh apples, pears, and peaches at the tasting room. RoxyAnn's former owner, Jack Day, is the son of John Day, the cattle rancher who built an airstrip on Lower Table Rock Mountain in 1948 to fly businessmen and Hollywood celebrities to the area. (See the Table Rock chapter for details). RoxyAnn's extensive wine repertoire boasts seventeen different bottlings, including Chardonnay, Sauvignon Blanc, Red Blends, Merlot, Cabernet Sauvignon, and a dessert wine made from pears! Drenched with dense flavors of cherry, blackberry, pepper, and spice, all strung together by supple tannins, RoxyAnn's Petite Syrah (a different grape variety than Syrah) will satisfy your thirst for Southern Oregon wine.

Petite Sirah: Petite Sirah is an offspring of Syrah. Known for its dense, rich fruit, sturdy tannins, and inky complexion, this wine is anything but petite, and pairs nicely with protein-rich dishes.

LAND MANAGER

City of Medford
411 W 8th Street
Medford, OR 97501
Phone: (541) 774-2000
www.travelmedford.org

WINERY

RoxyAnn Winery
3283 Hillcrest Road
Medford OR 97504
Phone: (541) 776-2315
roxyann.com
Distance from trailhead: 3.7 miles

LOWER TABLE ROCK TRAIL

LOOK OUT AT THE ROUGE VALLEY FROM A VOLCANIC PLATEAU

STARTING POINT	DESTINATION
LOWER TABLE ROCK TRAILHEAD	TABLE ROCK
WINERY	HIKE TYPE
KRISELLE	MODERATE
DOG FRIENDLY	SEASON
NO	YEAR-ROUND
FEES	DURATION
NONE	2 HOURS
MAP REFERENCE	LENGTH
POSTED AT TRAILHEAD	5.8 MILES (ROUND-TRIP)
HIGHLIGHTS	ELEVATION GAIN
UPPER TABLE ROCK	820 FEET

RED BLEND

DI'TANI

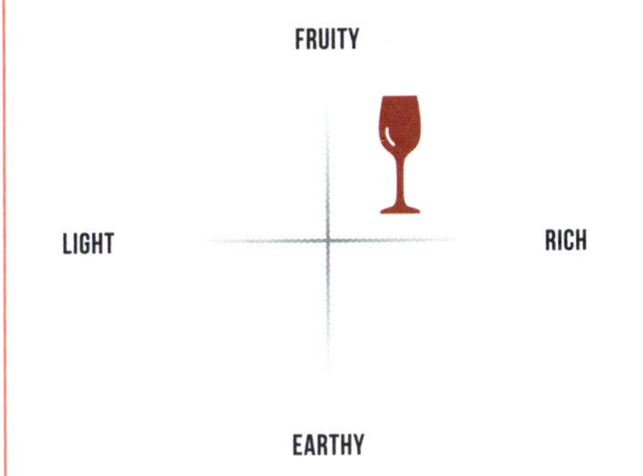

RED,
DRY,
STILL

DARK CHERRY,
RED FRUIT,
STRUCTURED
TANNIN, SPICE

RUBY

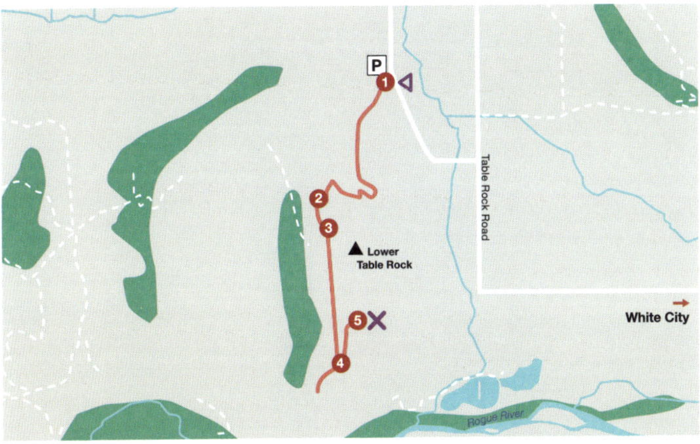

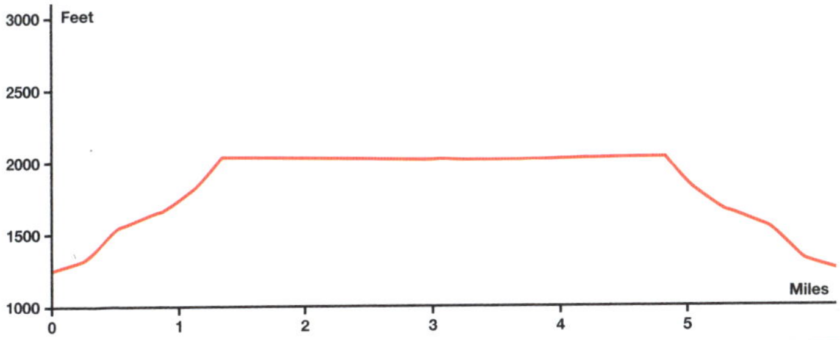

HIKE DESCRIPTION

Hike up a colossal table that looks right out of a sci-fi novel; then settle down for a little table talk and a special kind of wine tasting.

Hiking Table Rock makes you feel like you're in Sir Arthur Conan Doyle's novel *Lost World*. This iconic lava plateau is one of the most visited hiking spots in Southern Oregon. Roughly seven million years ago, Mount Olson erupted, flooding the valley with 800 feet of molten lava. Over time, the Rogue River has eroded most of the volcanic rock, leaving remnants in the form of a high rising plateau.

These volcanic mesas form a rich ecosystem dotted with vernal pools, making them an ideal habitat for the protected fairy shrimp. Table Rock is covered with expansive grasslands full of wildflowers that are home to 70 animal species and over 300 plant varieties. It is the only place on earth you can see the dwarf wooly meadowfoam!

In 1948, local cattle rancher John Day built an airfield on Lower Table Rock. The almost-mile-long runway attracted social elites and Hollywood celebrities, who were served up an impressive plane ride, a tour of the Rogue River, and the opportunity to buy prime real estate. Famed dancer Ginger Rogers often hosted Day's visitors at her Shady Cove

ranch. Though no longer in use, the remains of the airstrip are still there and form part of the second half of our trail.

The first mile and a half is a steady uphill walk through knotted madrones and arching oaks. The path splits at the top. The path to the left takes hikers along the eastern cliff edge, while the path that continues straight ahead follows the old John Day airstrip, leading to the southernmost ledge of the plateau with views of orchards, vineyards, Roxy Ann Mountain, and the snowcapped peak of Mount McLoughlin.

TURN-BY-TURN DIRECTIONS

1. From the parking lot, begin a steady ascent.
2. At 1.4 miles, reach the top of the plateau.
3. At 1.5 miles, stay right at the trail junction. Continue straight along the plateau (this section is the original John Day airstrip).
4. At 2.3 miles, reach the southernmost viewpoint.
5. At 2.9 miles, reach the eastern viewpoint. Return the way you came.

FIND THE TRAILHEAD

From I-5, take Exit 33. Head east on Pine Street to Table Rock Road; turn left on Table Rock Road. Follow Table Rock Road for 7.7 miles and then turn left on Wheeler Road. Follow Wheeler Road for 0.8 miles to the parking area and trailhead, which are on the left.

KRISELLE CELLARS

Southern Oregon is arguably the most diverse wine-producing region in the state. In addition to exceptional Pinot Noirs, it also cultivates a plethora of other exciting grape varieties. Kriselle Winery grows a particularly diverse array, including Cabernet Sauvignon, Sauvignon Blanc, and Southern Oregon's star: Tempranillo. Kriselle Cellars also produces a special blend known as Di'tani (De-Tawny), a native Takelma word that means "the rock above," and is a reference to the Table Rocks. In Oregon wine country, Kriselle is regarded as the quintessential family winery and tasting room. Pair your wine with one of the food offerings, which include blue cheese, kettle chips, prosciutto, creamy brie, and juicy olives. Be sure to stop by on the weekends for homemade pizza! Grab a glass of Di'tani and soak up the charm and allure of the Southern Oregon countryside.

LAND MANAGER

BLM Medford District Office
3040 Biddle Road
Medford, OR 97504
Phone: (541) 618-2200
www.blm.gov

WINERY

Kriselle Cellars
12956 Modoc Road
White City, OR 97503
Phone: (541) 830-8466
www.krisellecellars.com
Distance from trailhead: 7.2 miles

NORTH BANK HABITAT (COMSTOCK)

TREK AROUND THE ROLLING HILLS OF THE UMPQUA

STARTING POINT	DESTINATION
EAST ENTRANCE/ COMSTOCK DAY-USE	MOUNT SCOTT SCENIC VISTA
WINERY	**HIKE TYPE**
REUSTLE PRAYER ROCK VINEYARDS	STRENUOUS
DOG FRIENDLY	**SEASON**
YES	MAY–OCTOBER
FEES	**DURATION**
NONE	2 HOURS 30 MIN.
MAP REFERENCE	**LENGTH**
NORTH BANK HABITAT	5.4 MILES (LOOP)
HIGHLIGHTS	**ELEVATION GAIN**
OLD-WORLD WINE CAVES	1,045 FEET

GRUNER VELTLINER

ESTATE GRUNER VELTLINER

FRUITY

LIGHT

RICH

EARTHY

WHITE, DRY, STILL

CITRUS, GREEN TEA, GRAPEFRUIT, TANGERINE, WHITE PEPPER

PALE STRAW

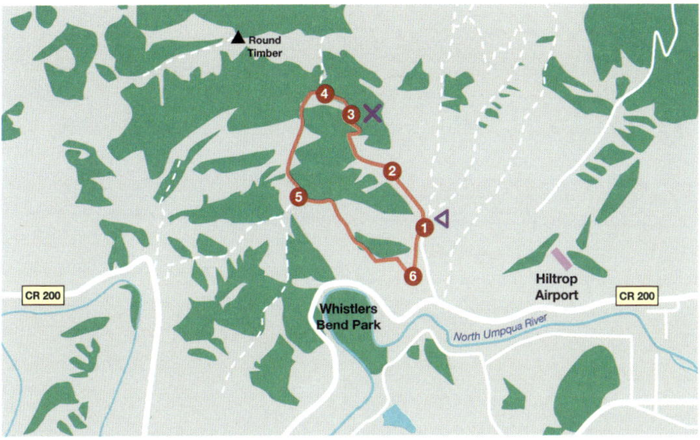

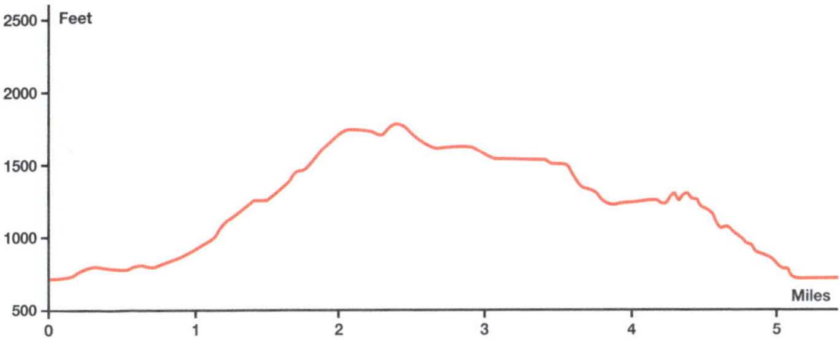

HIKE DESCRIPTION

Journey through a 6,000-acre wildlife preserve in Southern Oregon's Umpqua Valley. Then visit Reustle Vineyards with its welcoming wine caves and sample wine from the first Gruner Veltliner producer in the USA.

Within its 6,000 acres, the North Bank Habitat Management Area features a labyrinth of hiking trails with majestic views. This unassuming wilderness area is tucked away in the rolling green hills along the north bank of the Umpqua River in Roseburg, Oregon. The distinctive beauty of the region is apparent as you make your way along North Bank Road to the east entrance of the park, also known as the Comstock Day-Use Area. At the east end of the parking area, you'll find the Soggy Bottom Trailhead, the start of a 5.5-mile looping hike that follows four interconnecting trails: the Soggy Bottom Trail, the North Gate Trail, the Middle Ridge Trail, and, finally, the Thistle Ridge Trail.

The hike begins with a gradual ascent through pastoral meadows and reaches a well-marked crossroads in just under a mile. Proceeding left on the North Gate Trail, you'll climb moderately for just over a mile along a tree-lined path shaded by groves of mossy oak and madrone. After about two miles, the trail leaves the shaded tree canopies for unobstructed hilltop grasslands. Look to your right for startling views of the towering rocky crags of Scott Mountain. You'll be tempted to snap a photo, but save your phone's memory space, as the best views are yet to come.

The most difficult portion of the hike consists of two very steep stretches at the end of the North Gate Trail, just before you reach the summit and the junction with the spectacular Middle Ridge Trail. Upon reaching the 1,015-foot summit, take in the sweeping views of Umpqua's "Land of a Hundred Valleys." If you are the type of hiker who carries a small bottle of wine and a round of artisan cheese with you, this would be the place to uncork and enjoy the breathtaking views at a conveniently placed picnic bench.

Leaving the summit, you'll proceed left on the Middle Ridge Trail along a grass-swept hilltop that offers 360-degree views, stretching from snow-capped peaks in the Cascade Mountains to the coastal Callahan Mountain range, and taking in every rolling hill in between. After about a mile of gently rolling, captivating scenery, the looping trail turns left; follow the descending Thistle Trail back to the trailhead parking area. The gradual two-mile descent back to the valley floor is lined by massive bark-shedding madrone trees and features unique views of the snaking Umpqua River below. The outstanding scenery continues throughout the final stretch until you reach the grassy lowland meadows surrounding the trailhead. The North Bank hike is exceptional because of the commanding and varied views that make it clear why this bustling wine region has become so popular.

TURN-BY-TURN DIRECTIONS:

1. Begin at the Comstock Day-Use Area
2. At 0.7 miles, turn left onto the North Gate Trail
3. At 1.5 miles, arrive at the Mount Scott Scenic Vista
4. At 2.0 miles, turn left onto the Middle Ridge Trail
5. At 3.1 miles, turn left onto the Thistle Ridge Trail and proceed an additional 1.6 miles.
6. At the junction at 4.7 miles, turn left and head back toward the parking area.

FIND THE TRAILHEAD

From I-5, take Exit 129. The northbound exit turns left directly onto Old Highway 99. The southbound exit turns left on Del Rio Road and crosses over I-5; take a left on Old Highway 99. Proceed for 1.5 miles and then turn right onto North Bank Road. Continue on North Bank Road for 12.7 miles. Your destination is on the left, marked by a sign for the North Bank Habitat Management Area–Comstock Day-Use entrance.

REUSTLE PRAYER ROCK VINEYARDS

It was on a motorcycle trip through the Austrian Alps that Stephen Reustle, a young but successful entrepreneur from New York, was inspired to introduce Gruner Veltliner to America. Stopping at a local restaurant, Stephen requested his waiter "bring a bottle of the finest example of Austrian white wine." An avid wine collector, he was surprised to find that what the waiter presented him with was a wine he'd never heard of—Gruner Veltliner. Upon tasting it, he found it "simply sublime."

Many years later, after moving to the Umpqua Valley, Stephen realized that his property might be well suited for planting the classic Austrian grape. Taking a leap of faith, he planted his vines, which produced the first vintage in 2005. This vintage led to the first commercial bottling of hundred-percent Gruner Veltliner in the United States. Hundreds of medals later, and with critical acclaim from the likes of the *Seattle Times, Winepress Northwest,* and the *SOMM Journal,* Stephen Reustle might aptly be dubbed the "King of Gruner."

Owners Stephen and Gloria Reustle have worked tirelessly to bring into being not only their Gruner but also a breathtaking estate vineyard that crafts more than 20 award-winning wines. Nestled within the rolling hills of Southern Oregon's Umpqua Valley, the winery sits at the foot of dramatic south-facing hillside vineyards reminiscent of France's Burgundy and Northern Rhône regions. Also reminiscent of old-world Europe is Reustle Vineyards' elaborate network of wine caves adorned with sparkling chandeliers, stone columns, and Renaissance Art.

Gruner Veltliner: The most widely planted wine grape in Austria, Gruner Veltliner has gained increasing attention for making some of the highest-quality wines in the world. Pairing with anything from spam to curry, Gruner is an incredibly food-friendly wine capable of being crafted into several styles, ranging from acid-driven and crisp to sparkling and even rich and full-bodied. Under skilled winemakers, Gruner Veltliner can age for decades, and sometimes even half a century. Many of the best examples come from Austria's Wachau region, particularly those designated as "Smaragd," which means "emerald." Smaragd is a reference to the lizards of that color that roam the vineyards of Wachau. Gruner has several distant relatives; it shares a grandparent with Cabernet Sauvignon and is a close relation to the aromatic Gewürztraminer grape and the Pinot family.

LAND MANAGER

Bureau of Land Management
Roseburg District Office
777 NW Garden Valley Blvd.
Roseburg, Oregon 97471
Phone: (541) 440-4930
www.blm.gov

WINERY

Reustle Prayer Rock Vineyards
7612 Oak Hill Road.
Roseburg, OR 97471
Phone: (541) 459-6060
www.reustlevineyards.com
Distance from trailhead: 19.8 miles

NORTH BANK HABITAT MANAGEMENT AREA

A NORTH UMPQUA WILDERNESS ADVENTURE

STARTING POINT	DESTINATION
WEST ENTRANCE PARKING	MIDDLE KNOB SUMMIT
WINERY	**HIKE TYPE**
PAUL O'BRIEN	MODERATE
DOG FRIENDLY	**SEASON**
YES (LEASH REQUIRED)	YEAR-ROUND
FEES	**DURATION**
NONE	2.5 HOURS
MAP REFERENCE	**LENGTH**
POSTED AT TRAILHEAD	5.9 MILES (LOOP)
HIGHLIGHTS	**ELEVATION GAIN**
HISTORIC HANSEN CHEVROLET BUILDING	1,150 FEET

FUMÉ BLANC

ESTATE FUMÉ BLANC

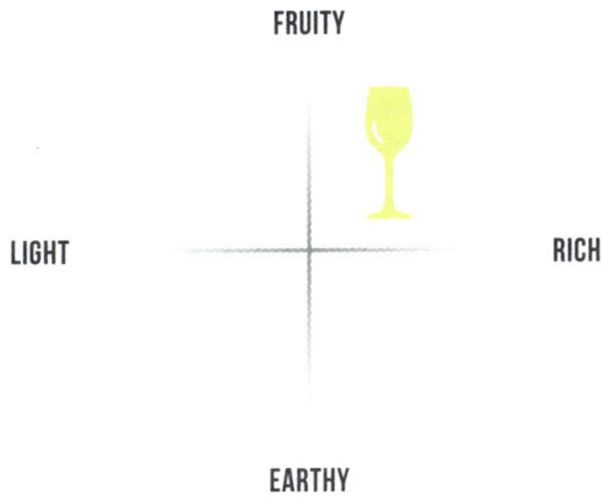

WHITE, DRY, STILL

CREAMY, PEACH, MELON

LIGHT GOLD

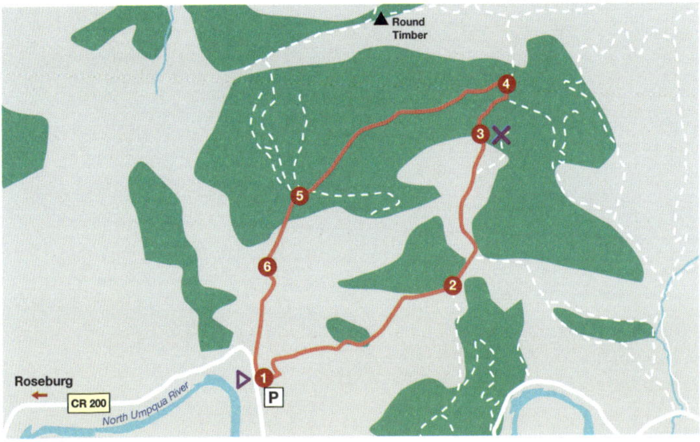

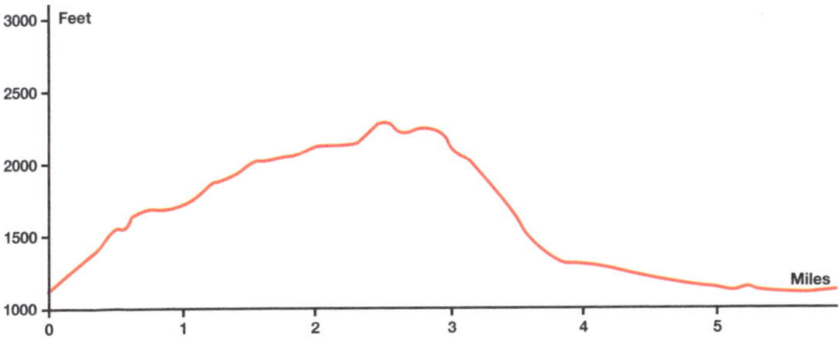

HIKE DESCRIPTION

Get a taste of "a place along a river" and then taste its wine at an urban winery.

A haven for the rare Columbian white-tailed deer, the Bureau of Land Management Habitat Area is a gem in the Umpqua Valley. The Umpqua Valley has become renowned worldwide as an outdoor playground for a wide variety of activities, including fly-fishing. The name "Umpqua" means "a place along a river" in the traditional native tongue, with several deviations in its spelling (Umquah, Umkwa and Umpqua). The river was officially bequeathed the name "Umpqua" by David Douglas (whom Douglas firs are named after), a horticulturalist working for the Royal Horticultural Society. Here, along the North Bank, you'll have the chance to hike through this "place along a river" and experience the untouched beauty of Oregon's oldest wine region. The rolling hills (reminiscent of Tolkien's Shire) are blanketed with madrone, oak, and an abundance of Douglas fir, which complement the majestic views of the Umpqua river as it winds westward between distant rises and ridges. In the winter and spring, the grass becomes so vibrantly green it reminds many people of Ireland. The area is devoted to conserving the Columbian white-tailed deer, whose population dwindled to barely 1,000 in the 1970s.

This hike is not to be missed when visiting the Umpqua Valley, as these trails provide no shortage of dramatic spectacles with possible sightings of red-tailed hawks, foxes, bears, and even the mighty and majestic bald eagle. Get a taste of the Umpqua Valley and its wine, perfectly paired with its idyllic scenery of forests, dramatic mountain ranges, and its crown gem, the Umpqua river glistening under the sun.

TURN-BY-TURN DIRECTIONS

1. From the parking lot, begin by following the Black Tail Ridge Trail.
2. At 1.5 miles, reach the junction with the Middle Ridge Trail. Go left and continue on Middle Ridge Trail.
3. At 2.6 miles, reach the Middle Knob summit. Continue on the Middle Ridge Trail.
4. At 3.0 miles, stay left on the Middle Ridge Trail.
5. At 4.6 miles, turn left onto Chasm Creek Road.
6. At 5.1 miles, stay left and follow the gravel road back to the West Entrance.

FIND THE TRAILHEAD

From Roseburg, take I-5 North. Follow it for 4.4 miles and then take Exit 129 toward Winchester and Wilbur. Continue for 0.3 miles; then turn left onto Old Highway 99 North and proceed for 1.5 miles. Turn right onto North Bank Road. Continue on North Bank Road for 5.4 miles. The parking lot and trailhead will be on the left, with a sign for the North Bank Habitat Management "West Entrance."

PAUL O'BRIEN

The collaborative efforts of Dyson Paul DeMara and his longtime winemaking friend, Scott O'Brien Kelley, resulted in Roseburg's first urban winery: Paul O'Brien. Housed in downtown Roseburg's historic Hansen Chevrolet building, the winery has a vintage aesthetic. In fact, the flooring is still that of the original automobile showroom of 1930. Dyson Paul DeMara was already a significant player in winemaking before co-founding Paul O'Brien. In 2003, he purchased Hillcrest Vineyards, the oldest estate winery in Oregon and the first to plant Pinot Noir. Paul O'Brien offers an interesting selection of wines, some of which are not typically found in the Umpqua Valley, such as the heat-loving Cabernet Sauvignon. While the winery focuses primarily on reds, be sure to try the Fumé Blanc. Fumé Blanc and Sauvignon Blanc are the same grape, but the name "Fumé Blanc" indicates that the wine has been fermented in a barrel (this name was coined by the famous Robert Mondavi and is a reference to "Blanc Fumé," Sauvignon Blanc made in the Pouilly-Fumé region of Loire, France). Fumé Blanc tends to be creamier and less sharp than typical Sauvignon Blanc (much like barrel-aged Chardonnay) and will occasionally display subtle hints of smokiness.

LAND MANAGER

Bureau of Land Management
Roseburg District Office
777 NW Garden Valley Blvd.
Roseburg, Oregon 97471
Phone: (541) 440-4930
www.blm.gov

WINERY

Paul O'Brien
609 SE Pine Street
Roseburg, OR 97470
Phone: (541) 673-2280
www.paulobrienwines.com
Distance from trailhead: 11.6 miles

COOPER CREEK RESERVOIR

ALONG THE CREEK, THROUGH THE WOODS, TO ABACELA WE GO

STARTING POINT	DESTINATION
WEST PARKING LOT	COOPER CREEK RESERVOIR
WINERY	HIKE TYPE
ABACELA	MODERATE
DOG FRIENDLY	SEASON
YES (LEASH REQUIRED)	YEAR-ROUND
FEES	DURATION
YES ($4 PARKING FEE)	2 HOURS
MAP REFERENCE	LENGTH
POSTED AT TRAILHEAD	5.5 MILES (LOOP)
HIGHLIGHTS	ELEVATION GAIN
WILDLIFE SAFARI	75 FEET

TEMPRANILLO

RESERVE TEMPRANILLO

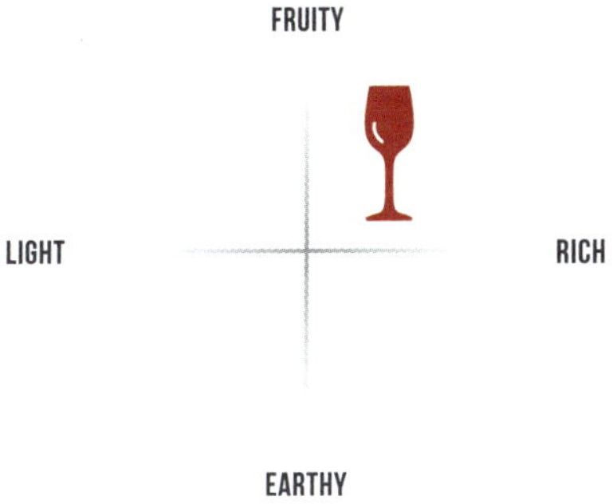

RED,
DRY,
STILL

SMOKE,
SPICE,
LEATHER,
DARK RED FRUIT

GARNET

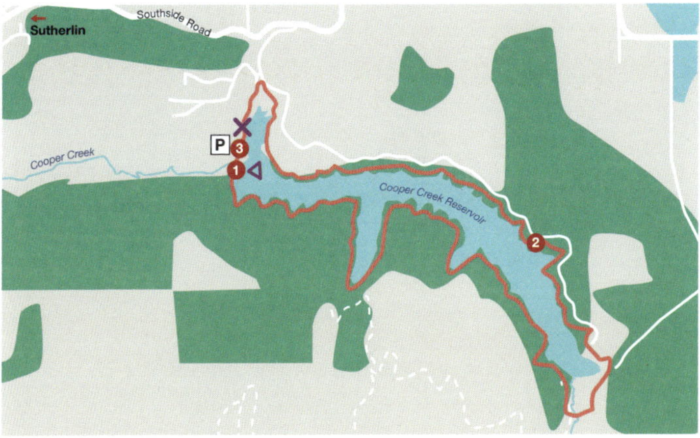

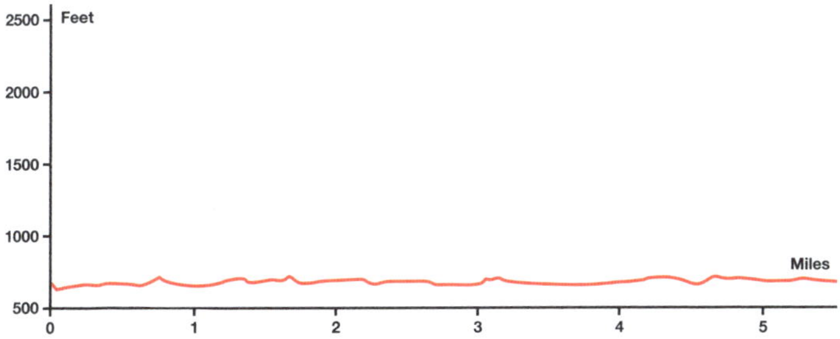

HIKE DESCRIPTION

Hike around a picturesque reservoir before enjoying a taste of Spain.

Sutherlin, named after the captain of the wagon train that traveled from Indiana to Oregon in the early- to mid-1800s, is home to a small reservoir that is a popular recreational spot with the locals, who spend many of their hot summer days waterskiing, jet skiing, fishing, swimming, and, of course, hiking. The Cooper Creek Reservoir Trail is a roughly 7-mile loop that goes all the way around the 166-acre reservoir. Since Sutherlin is only some 15–20 minutes from six different wineries, Cooper Creek is the perfect hike to take before a wine-tasting trip in the esteemed Umpqua Valley.

There are two trailheads at Cooper Creek. From the main parking lot, you can start at the Cooper Creek West Trailhead. The second trailhead is Cooper Creek East Trailhead, which you can access further down the road. Most of the hike weaves through forests of Douglas firs

that create a shaded oasis on hot summer days. The sound of boats and water-skiers will occasionally spill into the woodland groves as you traverse the higher ridgelines. You'll make your way through thickets of lush ferns and open meadows, from which you can catch sight of the sunlight glistening against the water—a delightful way to spend a few hours in a picturesque forest.

TURN-BY-TURN DIRECTIONS

1. From the trailhead, walk 100 yards from the Cooper Creek West Trailhead and cross the Cooper Creek Dam.
2. At 3.7 miles, pass the Cooper Creek Day-Use boat ramp.
3. At 5.5 miles, arrive back at the west parking lot and trailhead.

FIND THE TRAILHEAD

From East Central Avenue in Sutherlin, head east toward the city center for 1.7 miles and then turn right onto Ponderosa Drive; then turn right on Waite Street. Proceed for 0.4 miles and turn left onto Southside Road. Follow Southside Road for 1.2 miles and then turn right onto Cooper Creek Road. Follow Cooper Creek Road for 0.3 miles. Turn left onto Edgewater Drive. Proceed for 0.3 miles to where the road ends at the parking lot.

ABACELA

Founded by Earl and Linda Jones in 1994, Abacela Winery ("abacela" means "to plant a vine" in Spanish) has become the leader of the Oregon Tempranillo movement. Through his research, Earl became convinced that the Umpqua Valley had the ideal climate for growing world-class Tempranillo—and he was right. Abacela's Tempranillo took first place at the San Francisco International Wine Competition in 2001, beating all the Spanish entries! Abacela also became the first American winery to win a gold medal in Spain's Tempranillo al Mundo wine competition. So, it's safe to say that Abacela deserves a mention in a book about Oregon Wine.

In 2021, Earl's son, Dr. Greg Jones, a world-renowned climatologist, took the helm at Abacela to continue its long-standing tradition of making world-class wine. But Abacela has another viticulture story, which dates to well over a century ago. The Jones family recently discovered several unknown grape vines among the blackberry bushes at the far end of their property. After doing some research, they found that the vines predated Abacela. In fact, they were 140-year-old Listán Prieto vines (mission grapes), presumably left behind by the Cox family, the original homesteaders on the property. In 2021, Abacela announced plans to harvest the grapes from the Listán Prieto vines, furthering its tradition of putting history in a bottle.

Looking for smoke, spice, dense fruit, and supple tannin structure? Abacela has you covered with its flagship wine, the Tempranillo Reserve. That said, there's no shortage of delicious wines for you to experience at Abacela. The team has experimented with dozens of other grape varieties—including Albarino, a Spanish grape known for producing lively white wines with mouthwatering acidity. And let's not forget to mention their food! Enjoy Charcuterie trays during the week, and don't miss the wood-fired pizza on Friday nights!

Abacela seeks to promote sustainability by donating hay grown on the property to the local Wildlife Safari. In return, the winery receives elephant manure from the safari village to use as fertilizer. This may be one of the few places in in the world where wine is nourished by elephant dung! Some claim you can hear lions roaring from the Wildlife Safari when you visit Abacela. To find out for yourself whether that's fact or fiction, grab a glass of Tempranillo Reserve, sit on the patio, and enjoy the spectacular views of the Abacela winery and the Umpqua Valley.

LAND MANAGER

Douglas County Parks Department
1036 SE Douglas Avenue
Justice Building, Room 116
Roseburg, OR 97470
Phone (541) 957-7001
www.douglascounty-oregon.us

WINERY

Abacela
12500 Lookingglass Road
Roseburg, OR 97471
Phone: (541) 679-6642
www.abacela.com
Distance from trailhead: 25.8 miles

WILLAMETTE VALLEY & THE COAST

SPENCER BUTTE

HIKE TO A PICTURESQUE SUMMIT NEAR EUGENE

STARTING POINT	DESTINATION
RIDGELINE TRAIL PARKING LOT	SPENCER BUTTE SUMMIT
WINERY	**HIKE TYPE**
KING ESTATE	MODERATE
DOG FRIENDLY	**SEASON**
YES (LEASH REQUIRED)	YEAR-ROUND
FEES	**DURATION**
NONE	1 HOUR, 15 MIN.
MAP REFERENCE	**LENGTH**
POSTED AT TRAILHEAD	2.1 MILES (ROUND-TRIP)
HIGHLIGHTS	**ELEVATION GAIN**
AUTZEN STADIUM	741 FEET

PINOT GRIS

DOMAINE PINOT GRIS

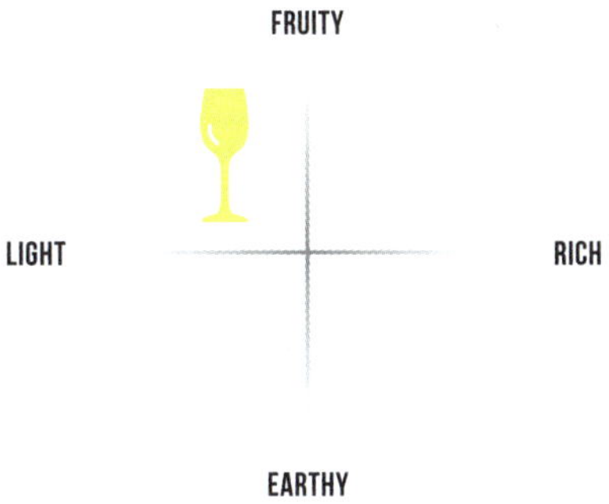

WHITE,
DRY,
STILL

TART PEAR,
STONE FRUIT,
APPLE

WHITE

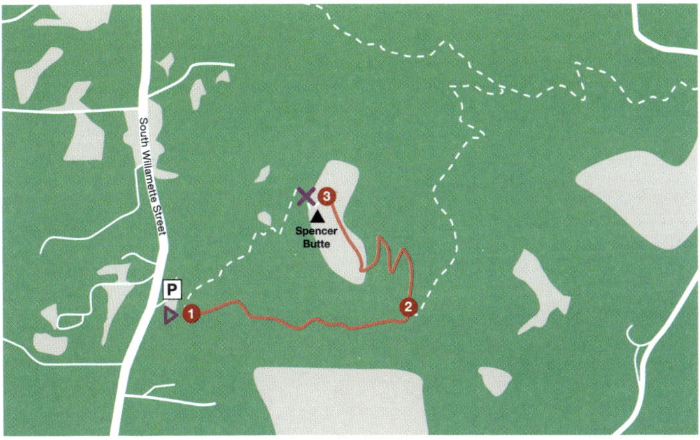

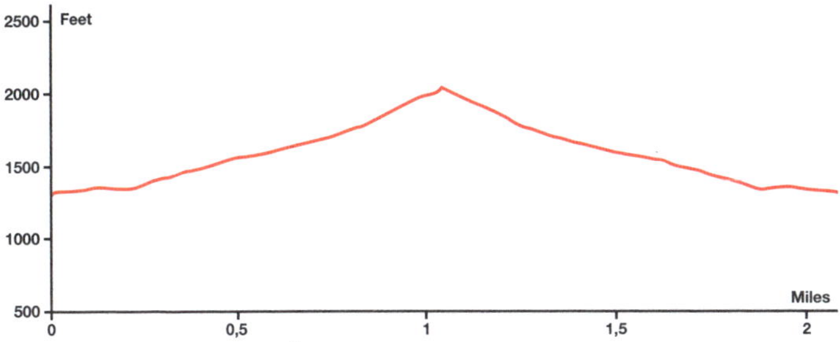

HIKE DESCRIPTION

You'll be king of the hill when you reach this summit. Afterward, enjoy royal treatment with a wine tasting experience at King Estate.

This scenic mountain trail ascends to the summit of Spencer Butte, just outside Eugene. The treeless summit affords uninterrupted views of Eugene and the southern Willamette Valley. On a clear day, you can spot Autzen Stadium, the home field of the Oregon Ducks, and the Three Sisters mountains. In the native Calapooya tongue, Spencer Butte was called Rattlesnake Mountain. Today, it's one of the most popular hiking adventures in the Eugene area. Two separate trails lead to the summit; to avoid a difficult uphill climb along rocky switchbacks, bypass the shorter trail that traverses to the left. The main hiking path, which proceeds straight, follows a more gradual incline to the summit along the western flank of the mountain, through a series of shaded forests. At just under a mile, you'll arrive at a trail junction; keeping left, proceed toward the final stretch on the eastern flank of the mountainside. The path leads you up a series of neatly cut stone staircases that take you to the bald butte. Upon arrival you can explore and climb several mounds of rock for panoramic views of Oregon's raw beauty. Return the way you came, avoiding the steep decline on the western side.

TURN-BY-TURN DIRECTIONS

1. The trail begins from the information kiost at the parking lot. Follow the sign reading "Main (Easy) Route to Spencer Butte Summet."
2. At 0.6 miles, stay left at the junction on the Spencer Butte Summit Trail.
3. At 1.0 miles, reach the summit. Return the way you came.

FIND THE TRAILHEAD

Take exit 189 from I-5 North. Turn left on E 30th Avenue and continue for 3.2 miles. Turn left on Hilyard Street and follow it for 0.2 miles; then turn right onto E 33rd for 0.5 miles. Turn left on Willamette Street and continue for 2.9 miles before turning left into the gravel parking lot marked "Ridgeline Trail."

KING ESTATE

Sometimes referred to as the New World counterpart of Burgundy, the Willamette Valley has become a world-renowned wine region. It is home to more than two-thirds of Oregon's vineyards and wineries. Among all these producers, King Estate Winery has emerged as one of the top destinations in Willamette Valley Wine Country. The largest biodynamic winery in North America, King Estate produces a diverse selection of wines and wine styles, including Riesling, Pinot Noir, Semillon, Tempranillo, and Grenache—and even some sparkling wines. The most notable, however, is King's Pinot Gris, which is bright, lively, and creamy. It's not just the wine you'll enjoy; the restaurant is delightful and offers an extensive gourmet lunch and dinner menu, served Wednesday through Sunday. The kitchen staff prepare dishes using estate-grown, sustainable, and organic ingredients from their 30 acres of gardens, greenhouses, orchards, beehives, and lavender gardens (from which they craft oil available for purchase). They also prepare a savory assortment of cheeseboards, cream tartar, crab cakes, fresh salads, grilled asparagus, and even swordfish. Enjoy spectacular views of neatly kept vineyards, orchards, and gardens poised against the backdrop of rolling hills, all while feasting on wine and culinary delights fit for a king or queen.

Pinot Gris: Commonly referred as Pinot Grigio in Italy, this refreshing gray-skinned grape is grown across the globe, producing clean, refreshing, and fruity wines. While the grape is often considered its own unique variety, Pinot Gris is actually a mutation of Pinot Noir. The mutation occurred in Burgundy during the Middle Ages, and it left the skins of the grape pale and incapable of making a red wine. However, Pinot Gris was found to produce high-quality white and rosé wines if pressed quickly and not allowed to rest on the skins long. It became one of the hallmark grapes of Alsace, a region characterized by its creamy and full-bodied wines with considerable depth. The Italian Pinot Grigios, however, are stylistically zippier and have a brighter personality than their Alsatian counterparts. Given the variety's stylistic flexibility, you might say there's a Pinot Gris for everyone.

LAND MANAGER

City of Eugene, Oregon
City Manager's Office
101 West 10th Avenue, Suite 203
Eugene, OR 97401
Phone: (541) 682-5010
www.eugene-or.gov

WINERY

King Estate Winery
80854 Territorial Road
Eugene, OR 97405
Phone: (541) 942-9874
www.kingestate.com
Distance from trailhead: 16.2 miles

MOUNT PISGAH SUMMIT TRAIL

TAKE A QUIET HIKE TO A SUMMIT JUST OUTSIDE EUGENE

STARTING POINT	DESTINATION
MOUNT PISGAH ARBORETUM	SUMMIT AND LOOKOUT
WINERY	**HIKE TYPE**
SILVAN RIDGE	MODERATE
DOG FRIENDLY	**SEASON**
YES	YEAR-ROUND
FEES	**DURATION**
$5 DAY-USE FEE	2 HOURS
MAP REFERENCE	**LENGTH**
AT THE TRAILHEAD	3.3 MILES (ROUND-TRIP)
HIGHLIGHTS	**ELEVATION GAIN**
THE THREE SISTERS, DIAMOND PEAK	1,000 FEET

MUSCAT

SEMI-SPARKLING MUSCAT

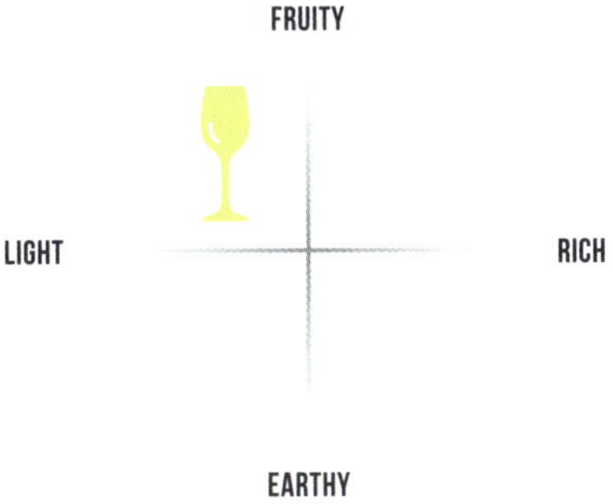

WHITE,
SWEET,
SEMI-
-SPARKLING

FLORAL,
RIPE PEACH,
CANDY,
MANDARIN ORANGE

STRAW (WHITE)

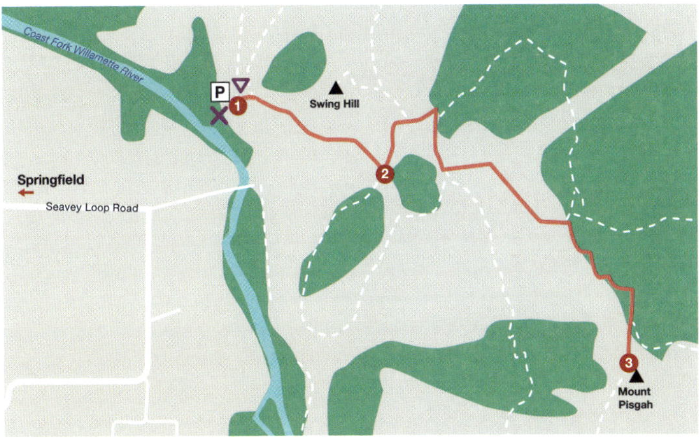

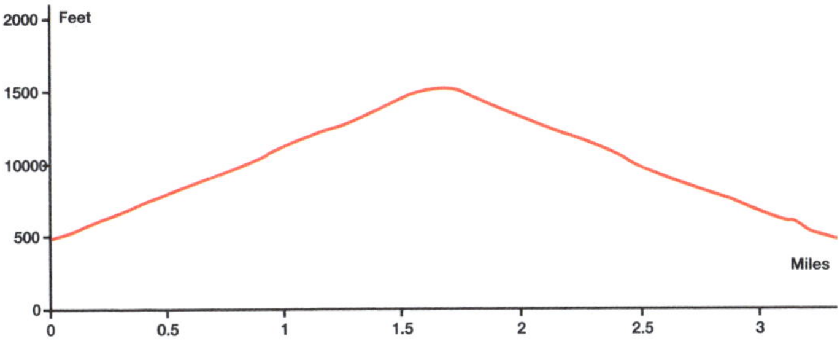

HIKE DESCRIPTION

Take a quiet hike above Eugene and then escape the city for some wine tasting at a hidden gem in the Willamette Valley's rolling hills.

This three-mile out-and-back hike will take you to a mountain top with charming views of the Southern Willamette Valley, Spencer Butte, Diamond Peak, and the Three Sisters. Located roughly ten minutes from Eugene, the Mount Pisgah Summit Trail hike is a gradual climb that winds its way through gently rolling hills cloaked with oaks, coiled madrone, and lofty pines. The crushed gravel path is wide and neatly maintained. It's ideal for walking in tennis shoes or for a moderate afternoon run to the summit. When you reach the top, you'll look down on the lush valley floor dotted with enchanting farms and vineyards. The park also boasts an arboretum and information center, where you can view several nature exhibits. At the trailhead and information center, you'll need to purchase a $5.00 parking pass from the ticket machine, which only accepts credit cards. Starting at the ticket machine, you'll begin a steady ascent along a gravel path. Several side trails crisscross the mountain, some of which interconnect with the summit trail. However, you'll stay on the "Summit Trail" (Trail 1) for this hike. Bring lots of sunscreen, water, and a good hat, as much of the hike consists of open ridgelines and grasslands with little or no shade. The final stretch provides slightly more shade as you trek through a grove of trees. But suddenly, you'll find yourself in the sun again at the open summit, where you'll be met by breathtaking views of the Willamette Valley.

TURN-BY-TURN DIRECTIONS

1. The Mount Pisgah Summit Trail begins at the parking pass vending machine above the parking area.
2. At 0.4 miles, continue on the trail as it turns left.
3. At 1.6 miles, reach the summit. Return the way you came.

FIND THE TRAILHEAD

From I-5 S, take Exit 189. Turn right onto Franklin Boulevard and follow it for 0.4 miles. Turn left onto Seavey Loop Road and continue for 1.5 miles until you cross a bridge. At the bridge, turn right to reach the main parking area.

SILVAN RIDGE WINERY

If you want to avoid the bustle of Eugene, look no further than Lorane. This small rural community may lack the grandeur of a big city, but there are several gems hidden among the hills and forests that surround this remote town. One such gem is Silvan Ridge Winery. As you arrive, you'll be greeted by a charming clock tower and quaint tasting room. Boasting several bottlings that run against the grain of typical Oregon wine, Silvan Ridge is the perfect place for those ready to taste something other than the standard fare of Willamette Valley—Pinot Noir. If you are open to trying something completely different, look no further than Silvan's Semi-Sparkling Early Muscat. Even if sparkling wine is not your favorite, you'll find that this wine delivers a distinct flavor profile that is completely different from Champagne or Prosecco. Sweet, bright, foxy, and slightly prickly (from the carbonation), this unique twist on the Muscat/Muscato grape is sure to refresh your spirits after a hike. The winery offers a cheese and charcuterie plate, a hummus plate, and a handmade chocolate truffle flight to enjoy with its tastings.

Muscat: Muscat (and its Italian equivalent, Muscato) is marked by its distinctive musky or foxy aroma. Found around the globe, Muscat/Muscato is produced in varying styles, including semi-sweet, sweet, and dry bottlings. More often than not, Muscat will taste no different as a wine than it would as a grape freshly picked from the vine.

LAND MANAGER

Mount Pisgah Arboretum
34901 Frank Parrish Road
Eugene, OR 97405
Phone: (541) 747-3817
www.mountpisgaharboretum.org

WINERY

Silvan Ridge Winery
27012 Briggs Hill Road
Eugene, OR 97405
Phone: (541) 345-1945
www.silvanridge.com
Distance from trailhead: 19.2 Miles

MARYS PEAK SUMMIT HIKE

ENJOY 360-DEGREE VIEWS OF WILLAMETTE VALLEY

STARTING POINT	DESTINATION
MARYS PEAK EAST RIDGE TRAILHEAD	MARYS PEAK SUMMIT
WINERY	HIKE TYPE
CARDWELL HILL CELLARS	MODERATE
DOG FRIENDLY	SEASON
YES (LEASH REQUIRED)	YEAR-ROUND
FEES	DURATION
YES ($5 PARKING FEE)	3 HOURS
MAP REFERENCE	LENGTH
POSTED AT TRAILHEAD	5.2 MILES (ROUND-TRIP)
HIGHLIGHTS	ELEVATION GAIN
PACIFIC OCEAN, MOUNT SAINT HELENS	1,450 FEET

CHARDONNAY

THE BARD CHARD

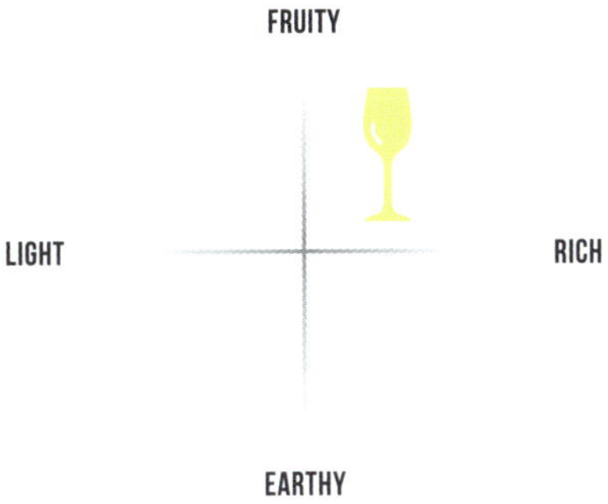

DRY, STILL

PEACH, CITRUS, EARTHY

LIGHT GOLD

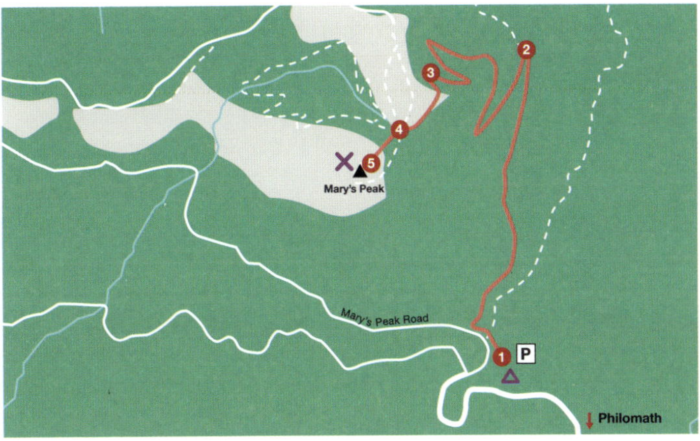

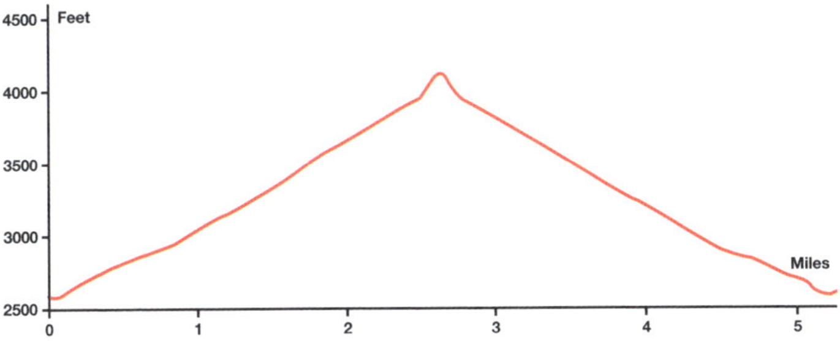

HIKE DESCRIPTION

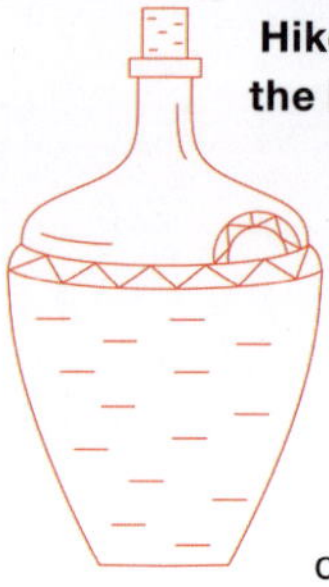

Hike to the tip of the Cascades and then drink with the Bard of Avon.

The tallest peak in the Cascade Coast Range, Marys peak (also spelled Mary's peak) provides views of several iconic landmarks. As the mountain is only 60 miles from the Pacific Ocean, the climate surrounding it can be unpredictable. On clear days, hikers can enjoy 360-degree views of the central Oregon Cascades, Willamette Valley, Mount Rainier, Mount Hood, Mount Saint Helens, the peaks of northern California, and the mighty Pacific Ocean! This hike features meadows of distinctive flowers like Oregon anemone, vanilla leaf, bluefield gilia, and the orange Columbian lily. The southwest face receives harsh winds, snow, and rain in winter and blistering sun in the summer, unusual climatic conditions that have made it home to a unique collection of subalpine wildflowers and high elevation perennial plants like the spreading phlox.

Though the summit is accessible by car (with a small walk to the top), the five-mile East Ridge #1324 Trail offers a more enjoyable adventure and better views. Starting at the eastern base of the mountain, you'll meander through forests and meadows before ascending the northern face toward the bald summit. (If you want a shorter hike, the upper parking lot joins the trail higher up and closer to the top.) As you near the summit, you'll suddenly cross the tree line and gain unobstructed views of gorgeous mountain terrain in Oregon and beyond.

TURN-BY-TURN DIRECTIONS

1. From the trailhead, take the East Ridge Trail #1324.
2. At 1.1 miles, reach the junction with the Tie Trail. Stay left on East Ridge Trail.
3. At 2.2 miles, stay left on the Summit Loop Trail.
4. At 2.5 miles, reach a trail junction. Remain on the Summit Loop Trail or head left on the gravel road to reach the summit
5. At 2.6 miles, reach the summit. Return the way you came.

FIND THE TRAILHEAD

From Corvallis, turn left onto Alsea Highway OR-34 West. Continue for 8.9 miles and then turn right onto Mary's Peak Road. Remain on Mary's Peak Road for 5.4 miles. The Mary's Peak East Ridge Trail (Conner Camp Trailhead) is on the right.

CARDWELL HILL CELLARS

Named the 2021 Oregon Winery of the year by *Great Northwest Wine Magazine* (formerly *Wine Press Northwest*), Cardwell Hill Cellars is a winery well worth visiting. It was purchased by Dan and Nancy Chapel in 2000. Dan has degrees in both chemistry and chemical engineering, so it's no surprise that he crafts some of Oregon's finest wines. Located in the foothills of the Cascades with a view of Marys Peak, Cardwell Hill Cellars is in an ideal location for making cool-climate wines. Utilizing sustainable viticulture practices, the winery produces roughly 8,000 cases per year, consisting of several different clones of Pinot Noir as well as bottlings of Pinot Gris and Chardonnay. Inspired by the Oregon Shakespeare Festival, the "Bard Chard" (Chardonnay), which features a portrait of Shakespeare (the Bard) on its label, is a great example of a Willamette Valley wine. With a well-integrated oak treatment, the Bard Chard highlights the more fruity and zippy qualities of Chardonnay that would otherwise be overwhelmed by oak. It is polished and smooth, comparable to a Burgundian Chardonnay. If the Bard is unavailable, the Pinot Noir Reserve is a delicious alternative to enjoy after a hike up Marys Peak.

LAND MANAGER

Forest Headquarters
3200 SW Jefferson Way
Corvallis, OR 97331
Phone: (541) 750-7000
www.fs.usda.gov

WINERY

Cardwell Hill Cellars
24241 Cardwell Hill Dr
Philomath, Oregon
Phone: (541) 929-9463
www.cardwellhillwine.com
Distance from trailhead: 20 miles

BALD HILL

FROM FARM LIFE TO WINE LIFE

STARTING POINT	DESTINATION
OAK CREEK TRAILHEAD	BALD HILL BARN
WINERY	**HIKE TYPE**
LUMOS WINE CO.	MODERATE
DOG FRIENDLY	**SEASON**
YES (LEASH REQUIRED)	YEAR-ROUND
FEES	**DURATION**
NONE	1.5 HOURS
MAP REFERENCE	**LENGTH**
POSTED AT TRAILHEAD	3.4 MILES (LOOP)
HIGHLIGHTS	**ELEVATION GAIN**
100-YEAR-OLD BARN	400 FEET

ALIGOTÉ

TEMPERANCE HILL ALIGOTÉ

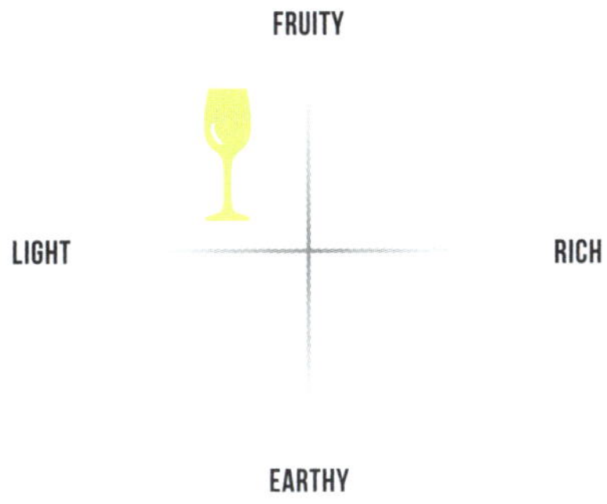

WHITE,
DRY,
STILL

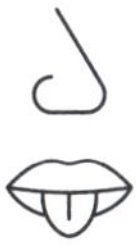

WET GRASS,
GRAPFRUIT,
LEMON

PALE STRAW

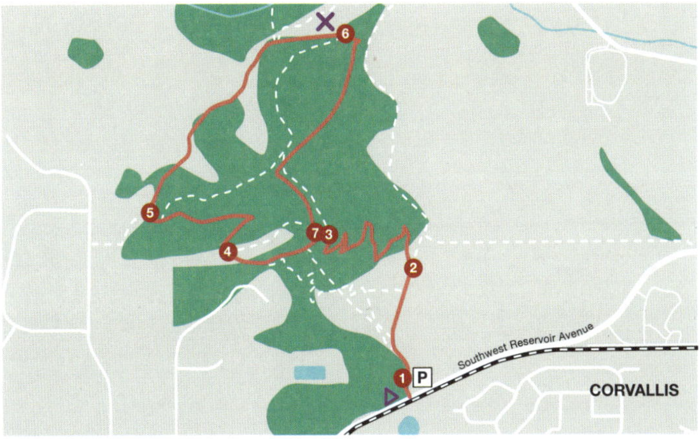

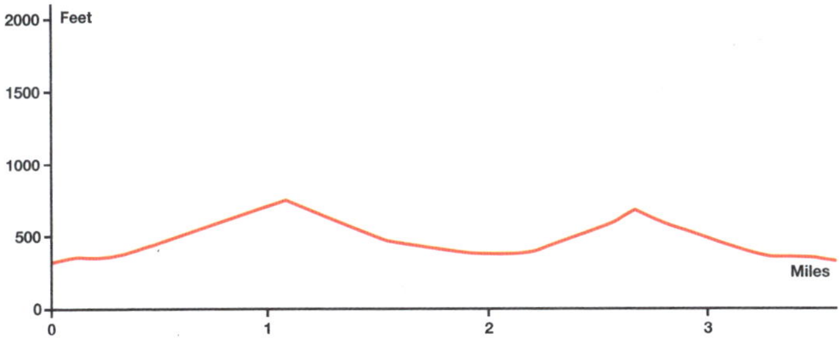

HIKE DESCRIPTION

Visit Bald Hill Natural Area for a countryside hike followed by wine tasting in a 100-year-old barn.

The Bald Hill Natural Area is located ten minutes outside of Corvallis Area, where urban segues into rural. Several trails cross the quaint rolling hills and gentle pastures along the perimeter of the Bald Hill Summit, where you'll have expansive views of Willamette Valley Wine Country. To the west, there are picturesque views of the far-off Coastal Range and the outline of its tallest mountain, Marys Peak. Bald Hill is void of trees and provides unobstructed vistas of the foothills and quaint farmlands of the Corvallis area. Surrounded by meadows, vibrant wildflowers and twisted oaks, the rustic Big Barn (part of the farm that was once located here) is a local landmark and the highlight of this enjoyable Oregon countryside hike.

TURN-BY-TURN DIRECTIONS

1. From the trailhead, proceed along the Bald Hill Multi-Use Path.
2. At 0.3 miles, reach a junction. Turn left onto the East Summit Trail.
3. At 0.8 miles, remain left at the junction and pass Summit Road.
4. At 1.1 miles, arrive at the junction with the West Summit Trail.
5. At 1.5 miles, bear right onto the Oak Savanna Trail.
6. At 2.1 miles, arrive at Bald Hill Barn and the junction with Summit Road. Turn right on Summit Road.
7. At 2.7 miles, reach the junction with the East Summit Trail. Turn left on the East Summit Trail and follow it back to the parking lot.

FIND THE TRAILHEAD

From Corvallis, head south on Southwest 4th Street/Pacific Highway for 0.5 miles. Keep right and continue for 2.4 miles on US20/West 4. Turn right onto Southwest 53rd and proceed for 0.4 miles. At the traffic circle, take the third exit and proceed for 0.1 miles before turning onto West Hills Road/Southwest West Hills Road. Continue for 1.1 miles. Turn right onto Southwest Reservoir Avenue and continue for 0.4 miles. The trailhead and parking area are on your left.

LUMOS WINE CO.

Voted one of *Wine and Spirits'* top 100 wineries of 2022, Lumos Wine Company adds magic to the Oregon wine scene. Harry Potter fans will associate "Lumos" with the magical spell that creates light in dark places, and Lumos Wine Co. certainly casts a light for wine lovers with its charming tasting room and selection of award-winning wines. The tasting room captures the Oregon spirit: it's in a renovated 100-year-old barn with polished hardwood floors and exposed beams. This century-old barn was originally called the H Bar H Dude Ranch and was a remote horse-riding getaway. Back in the day, visitors could rent the ranch house and cabins, ride horses, go to the daily dance at the lodge, and even have dinners made from fresh produce grown on the property.

Mild summers, caused by the influx of cool air from the coast, allow the vines here to ripen their fruit slowly, preserving their natural acidity and concentrating layers of delicate flavor and color compounds—essential elements for delicious wines. Lumos offers several bottlings of Pinot Gris, Sauvignon Blanc, and the less common but intriguing Aligoté grape. Acid hounds, Aligoté is for you. If you've never tasted the grape, this white wine is light-bodied and led by a racing acidity; it makes a harmonious pairing with spicy Asian cuisine and buttery seafood. Some of its more notable characteristics are green apple, lemon, and freshly cut wet grass. With a tasting barn situated against the misty backdrop of Oregon's Coastal Range and thick forests overlooking its neatly trimmed vineyards, Lumos Wine Co. captures the essence of Oregon wine country.

Aligoté: Though not as prominent as its younger sibling, Chardonnay, the white variety Aligoté is one of Burgundy's "other white grapes." Aligoté is also closely related to Gamay Noir and typically produces tart, acid-driven table wines. It is sometimes even used in Burgundian sparkling wine. Aligoté is often mixed with blackcurrant liqueur to create the French cocktail "Kir." (Kir was named after a Burgundian priest who joined the French resistance during World War II.)

LAND MANAGER

Green Belt Land Trust
101 SW Western Boulevard, Ste. 111
Corvallis, OR 97333
Phone: (541) 752-9609
www.greenbeltlandtrust.org

WINERY

Lumos Wine Co.
24000 Cardwell Hill Drive
Philomath, OR 97370
Phone: (541) 929-3519
www.lumoswine.com
Distance from trailhead: 9.4 Miles

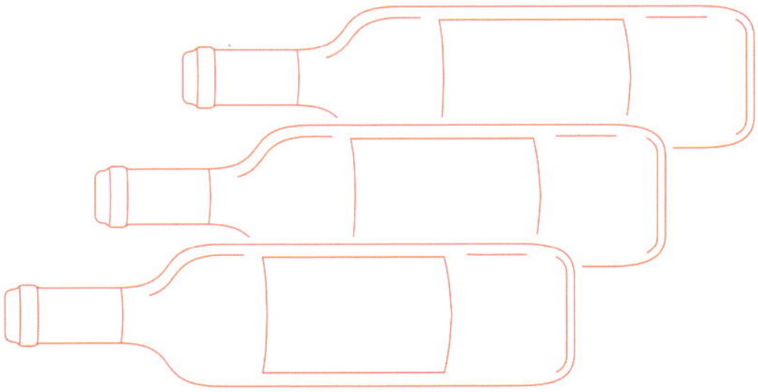

SILVER FALLS CANYON TRAIL LOOP

VIEW SEVEN WATERFALLS IN A SINGLE HIKE

STARTING POINT	DESTINATION
SILVER FALLS LODGE	SOUTH FALLS
WINERY	**HIKE TYPE**
WILLAMETTE VALLEY VINEYARDS	MODERATE
DOG FRIENDLY	**SEASON**
NO	YEAR-ROUND
FEES	**DURATION**
$5 PARKING FEE	2 HOURS, 30 MIN.
MAP REFERENCE	**LENGTH**
AT THE TRAILHEAD	5.1 MILES (LOOP)
HIGHLIGHTS	**ELEVATION GAIN**
SILVER FALLS LODGE	1,000 FEET

PINOT NOIR

WHOLE CLUSTER PINOT NOIR

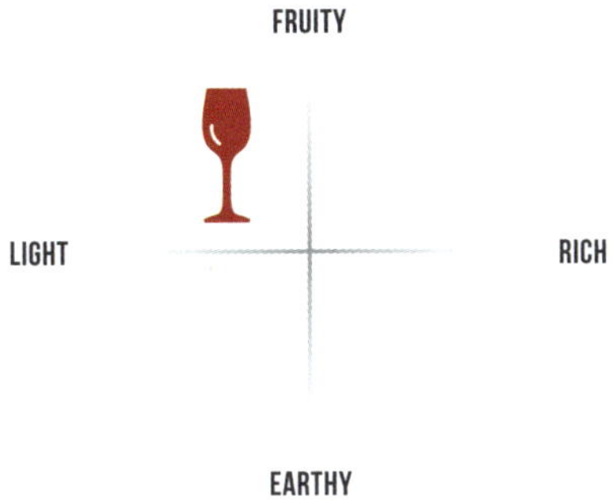

RED, DRY, STILL

TART CHERRIES, DAMP EARTH, STURDY

RUBY

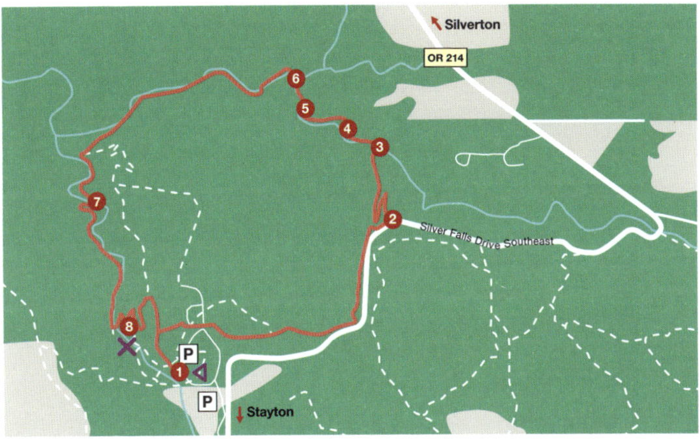

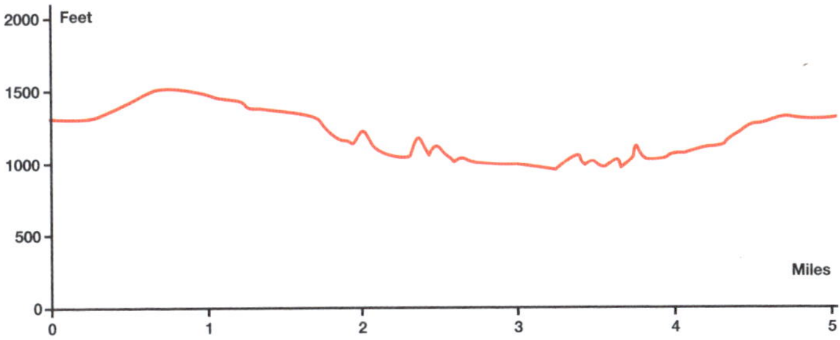

HIKE DESCRIPTION

Hike the Trail of Ten Falls at Silver Falls State Park; then visit the trailblazer of New World Burgundy in Oregon.

With its ten waterfalls, Silver Falls State Park is a popular destination for outdoor enthusiasts. Located just east of Salem, it's the largest state park in Oregon. This waterfall mecca was originally used by the Kalapuya tribe for hunting and spiritual quests. Silver Falls became an official state park in 1933 after the onset of the Great Depression. None of the waterfalls are named "Silver Falls"; rather, the name describes the ten falls of the park collectively. If it's summer and you don't mind getting a little wet, you can walk behind several of these magnificent works of nature for a light dose of refreshing mist. This classic Oregon hiking adventure is easily accessible, even in the cooler months. If you decide to visit in the winter, Silver Falls Café, where you can cozy up to the stone fireplace with a mug of hot chocolate, is a short walk from the parking lot.

Starting at the Silver Falls Lodge parking area, set off on a trail of paver stones. Following the Rim Trail, Winter Trail, and Canyon Trail, you can view seven of the ten waterfalls in the park. Many of these cascading wonders plummet from 100-foot moss-clad cliffs into glistening pools of foaming turquoise water. After heading eastward along the Rim Trail for about a mile and a half, you'll join the Winter Trail, which will take you to the first waterworks: Winter Falls. From here, the waterfalls become ever more impressive. After about another half mile, you'll leave the Winter Trail and strike off on the Canyon Trail. You'll soon come to Middle North Falls and, shortly afterward, the smaller Drake Falls. Each waterfall is different from the one before, and short segments between them lead through a forest drenched with the scent of fresh pine. After Drake, you'll come upon Lower North Falls. With only a mile to go, your hiking efforts will be rewarded with the grand finale: South Falls. At 177 feet, it's the most magnificent of them all. You'll then continue walking on the Canyon Trail for approximately five minutes back to the path you started on, which returns you to the Silver Falls Lodge info center and parking lot.

TURN-BY-TURN DIRECTIONS

1. Starting at Silver Falls Parking lot, proceed past the Lodge and stay right on the Rim Trail.
2. At 1.3 miles, turn left onto the Winter Falls trail.
3. At 1.8 miles, turn left onto the Canyon Trail.
4. At 2.0 miles, reach Middle North Falls.
5. At 2.2 miles, reach Drake Falls, followed by Double Falls.
6. At 2.4 miles, reach Lower North Falls.
7. At 3.7 miles, reach Lower South Falls.
8. At 4.4 miles, arrive at South Falls. Remain on the Canyon Trail and head back to the Silver Falls Lodge.

FIND THE TRAILHEAD

From I-5, take Exit 248 for 0.2 miles to Delaney Rd. Turn right on Delaney Road SE and follow it for 0.8 miles. Turn right to stay on Delaney Road SE for 2.0 miles. Turn right on 3rd Street SE and continue for 0.3 miles. Turn left on Denver Street SE. After 0.4 miles, continue straight ahead on Marion Road SE for 0.4 miles. Continue straight on Mill Creek Road SE for 3.1 miles and then head straight to follow Main Street for 0.5 miles. Turn left onto N 1st Street and proceed for 1.0 miles. Continue straight onto Shaw Highway SE for 0.6 miles. Continue straight ahead on Brownell Drive SE for 1.3 miles, then head straight again on OR-214 N for 11.9 miles. Take a left onto an unmarked road toward the Silver Falls Day-Use Area. Turn left again after 0.3 miles and take a sharp left after 400 feet to arrive at the Silver Falls Day-Use parking area and pay station.

WILLAMETTE VALLEY VINEYARDS

After a hike in the largest state park in Oregon, it's only appropriate to visit the state's largest winery. Washington State's Chateau Saint Michelle and California's Gallo produce millions of cases of vino, and Willamette Valley Vineyard is relatively small by comparison. But small, high-quality production is the Oregon way. Roughly 70 percent of the state's wineries produce fewer than 5,000 cases per year, and many are small family operations. Willamette Valley Vineyards has played a pivotal role in Oregon's quest to become the Burgundy of the Americas. Like all great things, Willamette Valley Vineyards had humble beginnings. In 1983, Jim Bernau began clearing the remnants of an old plum orchard near Salem. The winery he established there focused primarily on Pinot Noir before slowly adding other top-quality wines to its repertoire.

Visit Willamette Valley for tastings paired with delicious appetizers, including cheese trays, BLTs, soups, and creamy oysters! Lounge on the patio or walk along the terrace and tasting deck to soak up views of the distant hills cloaked in lush green vines. Cozy up to a crackling fire in the tasting room on cooler days as you sip a glass of Pinot Noir. The wine of choice is not just any Pinot Noir but a Whole Cluster Pinot Noir. What's that, you ask? While the method employs a traditional red winemaking technique, producers who use Whole Cluster are few and far in between. Most winery operations remove the stems from the grapes prior to fermentation. However, Whole Cluster wines ferment

the juice and fruit together with the grape stems. Winemakers decide how much of the stems to use. The resulting wines have a more sturdy woody texture that is sometimes even described as a chalky sensation. The flavor profile is probably distinct from that of most wines you've tried, but it is enjoyable and well worth trying if you're an adventurous wine taster.

LAND MANAGER

Oregon Parks and Recreation Department
20024 Silver Falls Highway SE
Sublimity, OR 97385
Phone: (800) 551-6949
www.stateparks.oregon.gov

WINERY

Willamette Valley Vineyards
8800 Enchanted Way SE
Turner, OR 97392
Phone: (503) 588-9463
www.wvv.com
Distance from trailhead: 22 miles

YAMHILL VALLEY VINEYARDS

A RIDGE WALK WITH STUNNING VIEWS OF THE APPLEGATE VALLEY

STARTING POINT	DESTINATION
YAMHILL VALLEY VINEYARDS TASTING ROOM	SOUTH PINOT BOOT BLOCK
WINERY	**HIKE TYPE**
YAMHILL VALLEY VINEYARDS	EASY
DOG FRIENDLY	**SEASON**
NO	MARCH–SEPTEMBER
FEES	**DURATION**
NONE	1 HOUR
MAP REFERENCE	**LENGTH**
TASTING ROOM MAPS	2.1 MILES (LOOP)
HIGHLIGHTS	**ELEVATION GAIN**
YAMHILL VINEYARD WINDMILL	178 FEET

PINOT NOIR

ESTATE PINOT NOIR

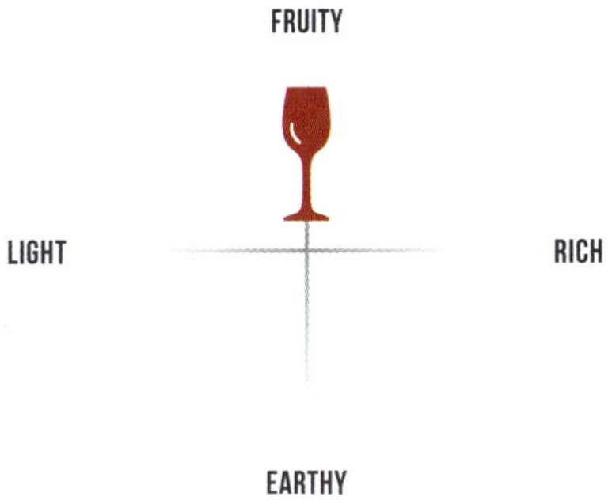

RED,
DRY,
STILL

RIPE CHERRIES,
JUICY,
VELVETY TEXTURE

RUBY

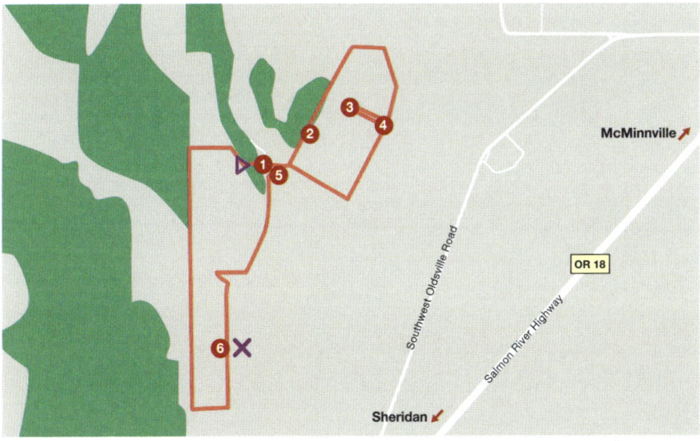

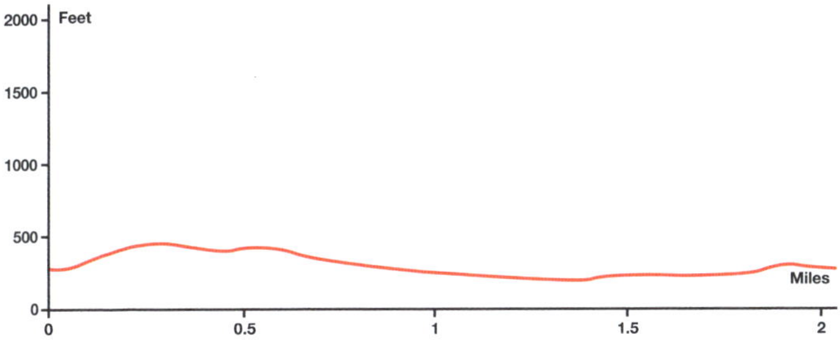

HIKE DESCRIPTION

"Wike" through vineyards and then relax with a glass of your favorite variety.

Most of this book features official recreational hiking trails, but since some wineries have popularized the term "wiking" (wine hiking) by opening hiking trails on their grounds, it seems only fair to recommend a few of the best ones here. In 2020, Yamhill Valley Estate established a 2.5-mile vineyard hike for visitors. It is an enjoyable and relatively easy stroll that winds along the vineyard roads. Follow the pink flags that indicate the trail and walk along open ridges and vineyard blocks planted with Pinot Gris and Dijon Pinot Noir clones. The vineyard blocks of Pinot Noir produce much of the wine you'll drink after the hike. Follow the trail back to the winery and experience a taste of what Willamette Valley is all about: yes, Pinot Noir. This trail is open daily from spring to early fall—call the winery for details. When you arrive, the tasting room staff will provide you with maps of the two vineyard trails. The first trail is slightly more difficult than the second and takes you along the upper end of the property. The second trail, which connects to the first, runs along the lower half of the property before ending at the tasting room. You'll need a reservation to do a tasting after the hike. Be sure to allow for 30–60 minutes of hiking (depending on your pace and which route you take) before your reservation.

TURN-BY-TURN DIRECTIONS

1. From the winery, proceed east to the corner of the Pinot Gris block and Orchard Road.
2. At 0.3 miles, at the top of the Pinot Gris block, head down the hill along the Pinot Noir Rainbow block.
3. At 0.5 miles, pass the windmill.
4. At 0.6 miles, follow the bottom edge of the rainbow block back to Orchard Road. Circle back to the tasting room.
5. Back at the winery, head toward the eastern side of the North and South Sequoia blocks.
6. At 1.1 miles, proceed around the bottom half of the Boot Blocks and up toward the western edge of the Sequoia block. From here, loop back to the tasting room.

FIND THE TRAILHEAD

From I-5 N, take Exit 228. Turn left and follow OR-34 W/Corvallis-Lebanon Highway 210 for 9.7 miles. Continue on NW Harrison Boulevard for 0.4 miles. Turn right onto OR-99W and follow it for 43.4 miles. Turn left onto SW Durham Lane and proceed for 1.1 miles. Turn left onto

OR-18 W. After 2.6 miles, turn right onto SW Oldsville Road. After 0.3 miles, turn left to stay on SW Oldsville Road. After 0.5 miles, turn right onto Yamhill Orchards. Reach the winery in 0.3 miles.

From I-5 S, take Exit 294. Merge onto OR-99W S/SW Barbur Boulevard/Pacific Highway W and follow it for 28.5 miles. Continue straight onto SW Baker Street. After 0.6 miles, merge onto OR-18 W. After 3.5 miles, turn right onto SW Oldsville Road and follow it for 0.3 miles. Turn left to stay on SW Oldsville Road and proceed for 0.5 miles. Turn right onto Yamhill Orchards and reach the winery in 0.3 miles.

YAMHILL VALLEY VINEYARDS

The oldest winery in the McMinnville AVA (American Viticulture Area), Yamhill Valley Vineyards is one of hundreds of wineries in the Willamette Valley that have helped establish Oregon as a world-renowned winemaking region. Dozens of stellar wine brands are scattered throughout the valley, and it's no surprise that sometimes smaller is better. Yamhill Valley has won numerous awards and was named the 2019 Oregon Winery of the Year by *Wine Press Northwest*. A boutique establishment, it focuses its production on world-class Pinot Noir. However, it also boasts several exceptional bottlings of creamy Pinot Blanc, crisp Chardonnay, and zippy Rieslings, all made from grapes grown in the estate vineyards. Yamhill Valley Vineyards also produces a Rosé of Pinot Noir. Grab a glass of whatever your palate fancies, relax on the deck, and enjoy a charcuterie tray paired with the picturesque scenery of Oregon's Willamette Valley after your hike along the vineyard trails.

WINERY & LAND MANAGER

Yamhill Valley Vineyards
16250 SW Oldsville Road
McMinnville, OR 97128
Phone: (541) 671-1657
www.yamhill.com

LEFT COAST CELLARS

STROLL THROUGH ANCIENT OAKS AND TRUFFLE SPORES

STARTING POINT	DESTINATION
LEFT COAST CAFE/ TASTING ROOM	TRUFFLE HILL
WINERY	**HIKE TYPE**
LEFT COAST CELLARS	EASY
DOG FRIENDLY	**SEASON**
YES	SPRING–SUMMER
FEES	**DURATION**
NONE	1 HOUR
MAP REFERENCE	**LENGTH**
AT TASTING ROOM	1 MILE (LOOP)
HIGHLIGHTS	**ELEVATION GAIN**
SPARKLING WINE CAVE	105 FEET

PINOT MEUNIER

PINOT MEUNIER BRUT ROSÉ

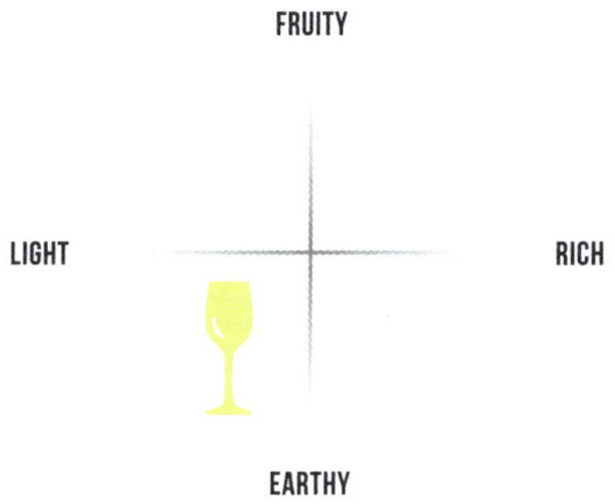

WHITE, OFF-DRY, SPARKLING

BUTTER, COOKIE CRUMBS, GRAPEFRUIT

COPPER, ORANGE

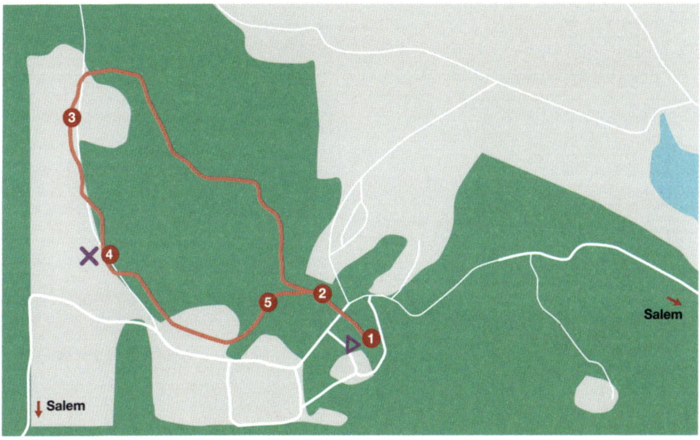

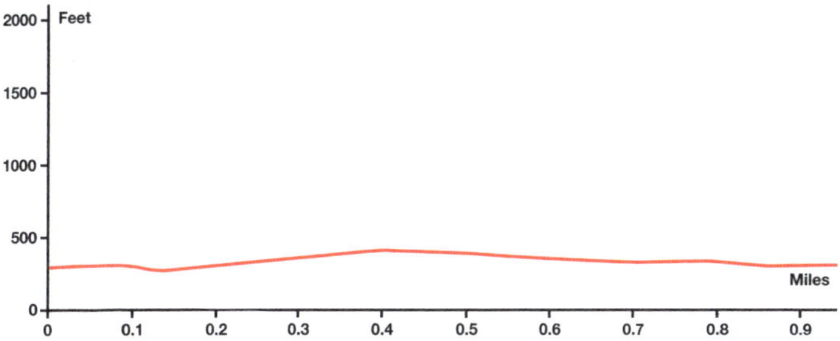

HIKE DESCRIPTION

Go "wiking" through the Oregon Savanna. Then add a little sparkle to your day with a one-of-a-kind Pinot Meunier Rosé.

Another winery to join the "wiking" movement (see previous hike) is Left Coast Cellars, located in the heart of the Willamette Valley. A delightful estate winery, Left Coast Cellars not only produces wine but also maintains a hiking trail that runs through its grasslands. With a focus on sustainability, the winery (in partnership with the Oregon Department of Fish and Wildlife) has devoted part of its nearly 500-acre property to the restoration of a native oak savanna. Some oaks on the property are roughly 400 years old, well predating Oregon's existence as a state. Left Coast has sectioned off and created a scenic one-mile hiking trail that runs through the savanna along the western side of its property. (Be sure to check in at the tasting room before going on the hike.) The path runs past Truffle Hill, where hazelnut trees have been inoculated with truffles: the roots of hazelnut saplings are doused with water and truffle spores prior to planting. (Oregon is one of the best regions in the world for farming European truffles.) The path then loops back to the tasting room and café, where you'll find refreshing wine, crispy wood-fired pizza, a warm ambiance, and premium hospitality, all paired with some "sparkle."

TURN-BY-TURN DIRECTIONS

1. From the tasting room, follow the sign labeled "Trailhead" and proceed across the oak grove.
2. At 0.1 miles, arrive at the gate and proceed along the cleared path to the left.
3. At 0.5 miles, arrive at the Pear Orchard.
4. At 0.6 miles, arrive at the "Truffle Hill" Vineyard Block.
5. At 0.8 miles, continue to bottom of Truffle Hill and remain right at the fork to reach the gate and trailhead.

FIND THE TRAILHEAD

From the Event Hall in Rickreal Farm Supply in Rickreal Oregon, turn right onto OR-99W N and proceed for 4.6 miles. Turn left and arrive at the winery gate. Continue for 0.8 miles and arrive at the tasting room and trailhead.

LEFT COAST CELLARS

Named Oregon's Top Tasting Room of 2017 by *USA Today* and the 2020 Oregon Winery of the Year by *Wine Press Northwest*, Left Coast Cellars is a must visit for any wine hiker. The winery devotes much of the production on its 150 acres of vineyard to Burgundian, Champagne, and Rhône Valley grape varieties: Pinot Blanc, Syrah, Pinot Noir, Chardonnay, and Viognier. One of Left Coast's most interesting wines, however, is a sparkling wine made by adding a small dose of honey (produced in the winery's own beehives) to the yeast to kick off fermentation and add some sparkle. And the flagship of Left Coast's sparkling program is its Pinot Meunier Rosé. Fermented in French oak barrels and aged in bottles with the yeast for two years prior to release, the Sparkling Pinot Meunier Rosé leads with notes of apricots, nectarines, grapefruit, and a touch of baked bread.

The winery also makes a red from Pinot Meunier that is a refreshing and juicy expression of the grape. The tasting room and café offer mouth-watering wood-fired pizzas, sweet and crunchy salads, cheese trays, and even dessert. The winery also sells duck and chicken eggs—truly a farm-to-table winery experience.

Running almost entirely on solar power and composting everything used in the vineyard, the winery prides itself on sustainability and restoration. Each year it holds a 10K called "Run for the Oaks," a fundraising effort to help the rare Oregon white oak from completely disappearing in the Willamette Valley.

Finally, you can schedule a wine cave tour and sparkling wine education experience for your visit to Left Coast Cellars. This is a perfect opportunity for anyone looking to learn more about the detailed process of sparkling wine production.

Pinot Meunier: Pinot Meunier, or Schwarz Riesling as it's called in Germany, is one of the main grapes used in traditional Champagne production. It functions as a blending component alongside Pinot Noir, Pinot Blanc, and Chardonnay. Because it typically ripens earlier and buds later than Pinot Noir, Pinot Meunier is an ideal grape for avoiding spring frosts and early autumn rain. A mutation of Pinot Noir, Pinot Meunier is mainly used in sparkling wine production, but can be used for making fresh, acid-driven red wines designed for drinking young.

WINERY & LAND MANAGER

Left Coast Cellars
4225 North Pacific Highway West
Rickreall, OR 97371
Phone: (503) 831-4916
leftcoastwine.com

MILLER WOODS

ENJOY A WOODLAND HIKE AND TASTE SOME WINE IN A 1920S RAILWAY STATION

STARTING POINT	DESTINATION
OUTER LOOP TRAILHEAD	MILLER WOODS POND
WINERY	HIKE TYPE
KEN WRIGHT CELLARS	EASY
DOG FRIENDLY	SEASON
NO	YEAR-ROUND
FEES	DURATION
NONE	2 HOURS
MAP REFERENCE	LENGTH
YAMHILLSWCD.ORG	4.1 MILES (LOOP)
HIGHLIGHTS	ELEVATION GAIN
1920S HISTORIC RAILWAY STATION	500 FEET

PINOT NOIR

BRYCE VINEYARD PINOT NOIR

DRY, STILL

DARK FRUIT, BLUBERRIES, WET EARTH

DARK RUBY

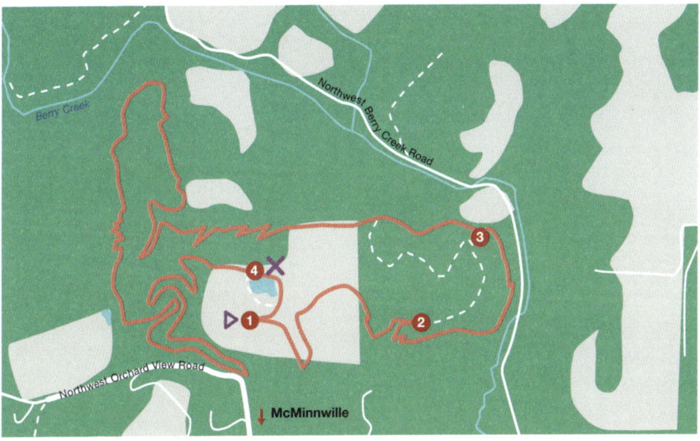

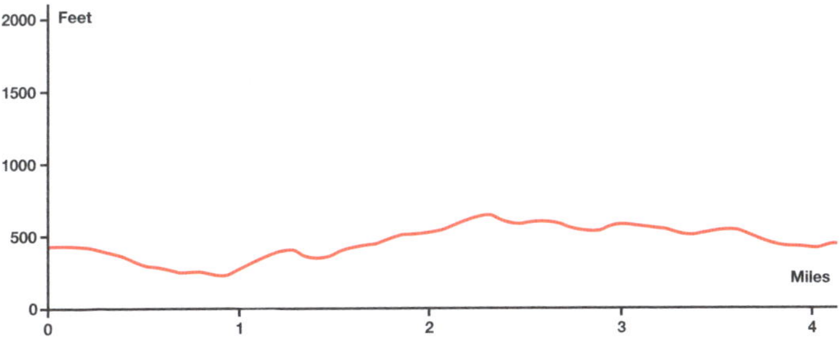

HIKE DESCRIPTION

Take a hike in Miller Woods and then catch the history train with a tasting at a 1920s railway station.

The Miller Woods Conservation Area is nestled in the heart of Willamette Valley wine country. Entrusted to the Yamhill Water and Soil District by K.T. Miller and his wife Frieda in 2004, the Miller Woods Conservation Area is ideal if you're looking to explore Oregon's natural beauty and then taste some of the state's finest wines. A 15-minute drive from McMinnville and 20 minutes from the Yamhill Carlton area, this 131-acre preserve contains several hiking paths that traverse savanna grasslands and quaint forest woodlands composed of yew, oak, Douglas fir, and cedar. There are also two charming ponds decorated with cattails and brightly colored flowers. Miller Woods is as quiet as it is beautiful. You may catch glimpses of wildlife, including otters, beavers, geese, deer, and porcupines. The US Department of Fish and Wildlife takes hundreds of trees, plants, and shrubs from Miller Woods and transplants them across the state of Oregon to preserve and promote the natural beauty and ecological richness of the "Beaver State."

TURN-BY-TURN DIRECTIONS

1. From the trailhead, take the Outer Loop Trail towards the meadow.
2. At 0.6 miles, reach the junction with the Oak Summit Trail and stay right on the Outer Loop Trail.
3. At 1.1 miles, and again at 1.3 miles, meet the Oak Summit Trail but remain on the Outer Loop Trail.
4. At 4.0 miles, reach the trail that circles the pond. Follow the path for an additional 0.1 miles back to the trailhead.

FIND THE TRAILHEAD

From McMinnville, take NE Baker Street North for 0.6 miles before turning left onto North Baker Street. Proceed for 0.3 miles and then turn left onto Northwest Baker Creek Road. Continue for 1.5 miles on Northwest Baker Creek Road. At the traffic circle with the Willie Nelson Sculpture, continue straight on NW Baker Creek Road and proceed for 1.3 miles. The road will split; remain straight on Northwest Orchard View Road for 0.2 miles. Turn right and stay on Northwest Orchard View Road for an additional 0.8 miles. Turn right again and stay on Northwest Orchard View Road for 0.9 miles before taking a slight right and arriving at the Miller Woods Conservation Area parking lot. The trailhead is on the right.

KEN WRIGHT CELLARS

Ken Wright grew up in a land flowing with bourbon and moonshine; he dropped his college major in political science and instead turned to wine. His introduction to the beverage to which he would devote his life took place in a small restaurant in Lexington, Kentucky. After taking wine appreciation classes with his roommate and planting some vines in the humid Kentucky climate, Ken decided to move to California and enroll at UC Davis. Here, he began rubbing elbows with some of California's most esteemed winemaking veterans. He became fascinated with Oregon wine and turned his sights toward the Willamette Valley, where his old roommate from Kentucky had become the vineyard manager for the famed Knudsen Erath. Utilizing innovative winemaking techniques that have since become standard in the industry, Ken contributed greatly to the development of Oregon winemaking. Ken's Abbott Claim Vineyard Pinot Noir was judged the #1 wine in the world by *Wine Enthusiast* in 2012. A few years later, Ken became the first Oregon winemaker to be featured on the cover of *Wine Spectator*. History buffs and winos alike will be delighted by Ken Wright's tasting room in the historic 1920s Carlton railway station.

LAND MANAGER

Yamhill Soil & Water Conservation District
2200 SW 2nd Street
McMinnville, Oregon 97128
Phone: (503) 472-6403
www.yamhillswcd.org

WINERY

Ken Wright Cellars
120 N Pine Street
Carlton, OR 97111
Phone: (503) 852-7010
www.kenwrightcellars.com
Distance from trailhead: 10.4 miles

TRAPPIST ABBEY GUADALUPE LOOP

VISIT A MODERN ABBEY AND SAMPLE PRESIDENTIAL WINES

STARTING POINT	DESTINATION
TRAPPIST ABBEY	VANTAGE POINT
WINERY	**HIKE TYPE**
ARGYLE WINERY	MODERATE
DOG FRIENDLY	**SEASON**
NO	YEAR-ROUND
FEES	**DURATION**
NONE	2 HOURS
MAP REFERENCE	**LENGTH**
POSTED ON WEBSITE AND TRAILHEAD	4 MILES (LOOP)
HIGHLIGHTS	**ELEVATION GAIN**
THANK-YOU LETTERS FROM THE WHITE HOUSE	673 FEET

VINTAGE BRUT

ARGYLE VINTAGE BRUT

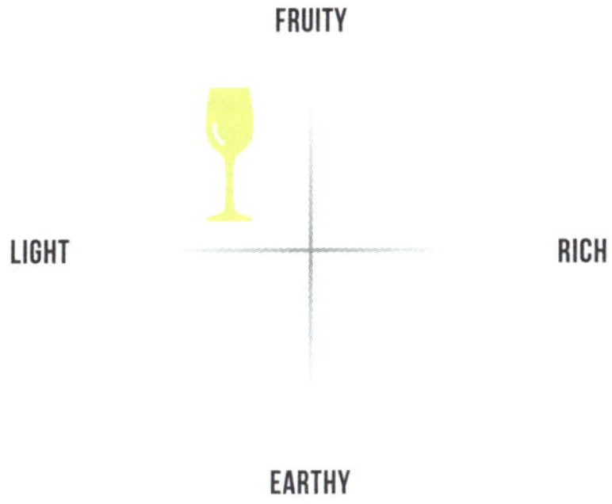

WHITE,
DRY,
SPARKLING

ALMOND,
TOASTED BREAD,
LEMON

WHITE

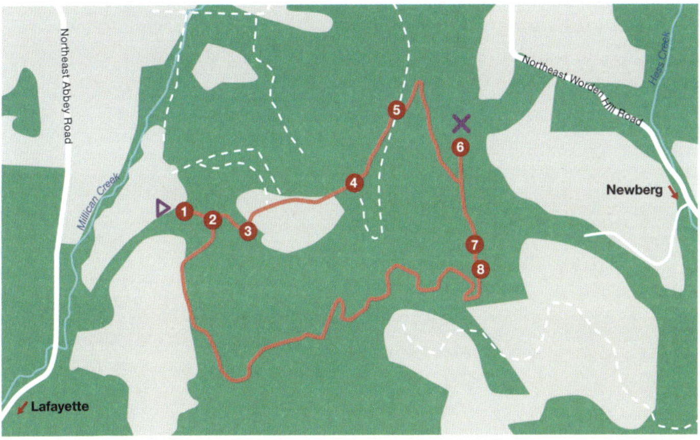

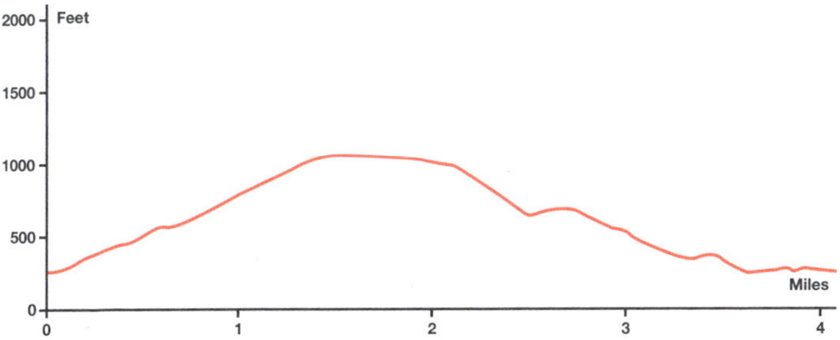

HIKE DESCRIPTION

Hike around a monastery and then sip a sparkling wine enjoyed by several US presidents.

While Europe boasts a plethora of brilliantly constructed monasteries, ancient ruins, and magnificent castles, there are very few places in the USA that have such attractions. That said, the heart of Willamette valley harbors something close. The Our Lady of Guadalupe Trappist Abbey is nestled among the rolling hills between Newberg and McMinnville. Founded in 1955 by monks from New Mexico, the monastery has a more contemporary and modernized feel than some of its European counterparts. But while the buildings and chapel are modern, you'll still feel the centuries of tradition maintained by the monks in the abbey, who operate a bookbinding business and a bakery specializing in traditional fruit cake. They also have a wine storage facility for local wineries and lease part of their land to local farmers.

Much of the 1,000+-acre grounds surrounding the monastery are devoted to conservation efforts. There are quaint forest paths running throughout the property, with the primary trail, the Guadalupe Loop, leading around the perimeter. The offshoots include the Monks Trail, Hermits Trail, Juan Diego trail, and Juan Diego Pass Trail. A vantage point at the eastern edge of the property will offer you charming views of Willamette Valley wine country before you complete the loop and return to the monastery. You can download a map of the trail network from the Abbey website. Be aware that no dogs are allowed and that the trails are open from dawn till dusk.

TURN-BY-TURN DIRECTIONS

1. From the trailhead, take the Loop Trail.
2. At 0.1 miles, take a left at the fork, remaining on the Loop Trail heading northeast.
3. At 0.3 miles, pass the junction with the Monk's Trail and continue on the Loop Trail.
4. At 0.7 miles, reach the junction with the Hermit's Trail and continue on the Loop Trail.
5. At roughly 1.0 miles, bypass the St. Juan Diego Trail and continue on the Loop Trail.
6. At 1.4 miles, reach a junction; stay left to reach the viewpoint, or continue on the Loop Trail.
7. At 1.9 miles, reach the Shrine of Our Lady of Guadalupe.
8. At 2.0 miles, reach the junction with the St. Juan Diego Pass Trail and continue along the Guadalupe Loop, which will bring you back to the starting point.

FIND THE TRAILHEAD

From 3rd Street/Pacific Highway West in Lafayette, turn right onto Bridge Street. This becomes Northeast Abbey Road after 0.7 miles. Continue on Northeast Abbey Road for an additional 2.3 miles and turn right to arrive at the Abbey parking lot and trailhead.

ARGYLE WINERY

One of the pioneers of Oregon wine, Argyle has been crafting delicious cool-climate wines since 1987. Located in the heart of Pinot Noir country, Argyle differentiates itself by specializing in sparkling wine. For its rosé, white, sweet, dry, non-vintage, and vintage sparklers, Argyle uses the traditional Méthode Champenoise, allowing the yeast to ferment the wine inside the bottle rather than force-carbonating it the way soda streams do.

Located 15 minutes from the Trappist Abbey, Argyle's tasting room combines modern flair with a respect for tradition. Though the wine is crafted using a very traditional winemaking approach, the tasting room feels incredibly modern. The ceilings are constructed from exposed rafters and timber beams that were part of the original winery. An intricately designed bar made from Douglas fir adds a raw and industrialized flavor to the ambiance. Interestingly, before its founding in 1987, the winery was an old hazelnut processing and storage warehouse. Looking for some history? In the back of the tasting room hangs a series of letters from former US presidents! Why? Argyle was the first Oregon sparkling wine to be served at the White House; it was first enjoyed by Bill Clinton and later by George W. Bush and Barack Obama.

One of Argyle's most distinct sparkling programs, however, is its "Extended Tirage." What's extended Tirage? I'm glad you asked. This process involves leaving the yeast in the bottle for long periods after fermentation—in the case of Argyle, an entire decade. It is a lengthy and expensive method, but this extended contact with the yeast helps

enhance the flavor and refine the texture profile of the wine. This often makes for finer bubbles, tighter foam, and a creamier prickly sensation—a contrast to the sharper and more abrasive flavors commonly found in younger sparklers. Common tasting notes of extended tirage include freshly baked bread, mustard, toast, and even almonds... something every sparkling wine geek will go crazy for! You can taste their standard vintage brut, which is tart, bright, and youthful, but you might ask the tasting room staff for the extended tirage equivalent to taste the differences.

Sparkling wine: Synonymous with the French region of Champagne, sparkling wine is said to have been discovered by the French monk Dom Perignon when, to his surprise, his wine re-fermented in the bottle. In reality, however (much to the chagrin of the French), it was the English scientist Christopher Merret who detailed a recipe for sparkling vino decades before Dom Perignon's discovery. The process of creating sparkling wine is incredibly labor-intensive, often requiring extensive capital investment and long periods of time. To create the bubbly beverage, winemakers mix a concoction of sugar and yeast and bottle it with an existing still wine. The yeast consumes the sugar, thereby producing bubbles. Winemakers generally remove the yeast after roughly one to three years, but, as mentioned above, some high-end producers will age their wine for decades with yeast still in the bottle. Dead yeast might sound disgusting, but rest assured, these single-celled winemakers are responsible for a delicious and unique flavor profile.

Note: "Non-vintage" wine (wine with no year indicated on the label) is a blend of several vintages. Blending poor vintages with better ones can create a more consistent product, and sometimes even a great one. Vintage Champagne, however, as the name implies, is crafted only in the best years, and comprises only a miniscule three to five percent of all Champagne wine. Vintage Champagne is generally more expensive and is considered superior to non-vintage. However, the quality of the final product will greatly depend on the skill of the winemaker.

LAND MANAGER

Our Lady of Guadalupe Trappist Abbey
9200 NE Abbey Road
Carlton, OR 97111
Phone: (503) 852-0107
www.trappistabbey.org

WINERY

Argyle
691 OR-99W
Dundee, OR 97115
Phone: (503) 538-8520
www.argylewinery.com
Distance from trailhead: 9.1 Miles

CHEHALEM RIDGE

HIKE TO A "QUIET PLACE" AND DRINK WINE GROWN FROM VOLCANIC SOIL

STARTING POINT	DESTINATION
CHEHALEM RIDGE TRAILHEAD	IOWA HILL
WINERY	HIKE TYPE
COLENE CLEMENS	MODERATE
DOG FRIENDLY	SEASON
NO	YEAR-ROUND
FEES	DURATION
NONE	2.5 HOURS
MAP REFERENCE	LENGTH
POSTED AT OREGON METRO.GOV	6.3 MILES (ROUND-TRIP)
HIGHLIGHTS	ELEVATION GAIN
COLENE CLEMENS OLD BARN	700 FEET

PINOT NOIR

ADRIAN PINOT NOIR

FRUITY

LIGHT

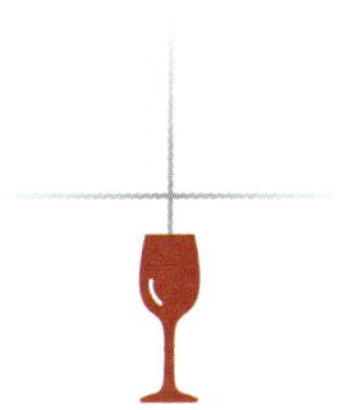

RICH

EARTHY

RED,
DRY,
STILL

BRIGHT CHERRY,
SUPPLE TANNIN,
SPICE

DARK RUBY

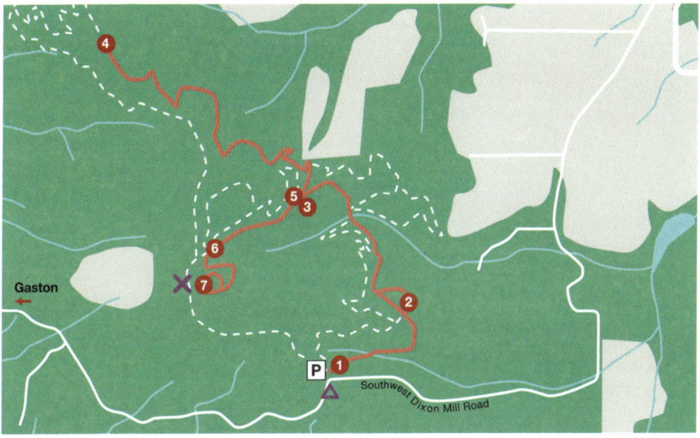

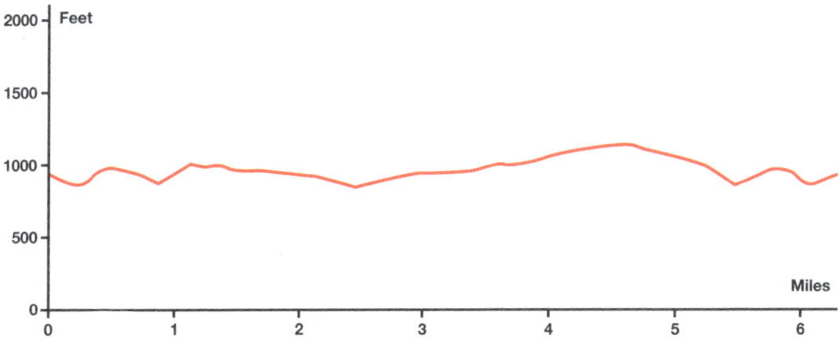

HIKE DESCRIPTION

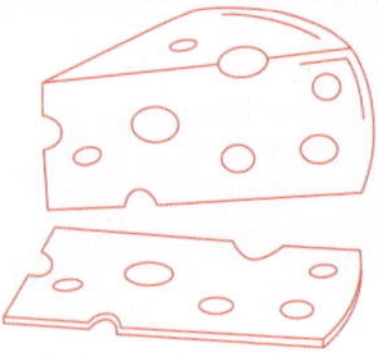

Hike through the Chehalem wilderness before sitting down to taste wine in view of Willamette Valley's highest peak.

Just south of Portland, nestled in the Chehalem wilderness, lies a 1,200-acre nature park. Chehelam roughly means "quiet place" in the Tualatin language, and on the Chehalem Ridge Trail you will indeed find quiet, as well as a picnic area and plenty of wildlife. There's no shortage of falcons, hawks, deer, and tiny hermit thrush. You'll traverse dense forests of old Oregon white oaks and madrone, and at the highest point of the park you'll come upon majestic views of the Tualatin valley and the distant Oregon Coast Range. You'll also encounter three distinct thin-plated steel sculptures: the Three Elders. These were created by the Confederate Tribes of Grand Ronde to serve as a memorial for their people, whose territory once included parts of the park. This confederation consists of over 30 tribes scattered across Oregon, southern Washington, and parts of northern California. The Umpqua, Calapuya, Rogue River, and Tillamook are just a few of the tribes that make up the confederation.

TURN-BY-TURN DIRECTIONS

1. From the parking lot, take the Chehalem Ridge Trail via "Timber Road" and pass the first Elder Statue, which marks the trailhead.
2. At 0.4 miles, turn right onto the Ammefu Trail to see the second Elder Statue. Then return to Timber Road.
3. At 1.1 miles, turn right onto the Chehalem Ridge Trail.
4. At 2.5 miles, reach a fork and turn back.
5. At 3.8 miles, turn right onto Timber Road (on your way back).
6. At 4.1 miles, stay left and take the Mampa trail
7. At 4.5 miles, reach the outlook on Iowa Hill with a lone oak and the final Elder Statue. Return along Timber Road (bypassing the Chehalem Ridge Trail).

FIND THE TRAILHEAD

In Newberg, head north on Main Street. Turn left onto Route 240/West Illinois Street. Continue for 5.1 miles. Turn right onto Northeast Ribbon Ridge Road and proceed for 0.8 miles. Bear left and follow Northeast North Valley Road for 3.8 miles. At the intersection with Northeast Laughlin Road and Northeast Albertson Road, continue straight on Northeast Spring Hill Road for 4.5 miles. Turn right onto Southwest Gaston Road. After 400 feet, Southwest Gaston Road turns left and becomes Southwest Hardebeck Road. Proceed for 500 feet and turn right on Southwest Dixon Mill Road. Continue for 2.5 miles. The parking area and trailhead are on the left.

COLENE CLEMENS

When Joe and Vicki Stark purchased an old homestead just west of the Chehalem mountains, they had no idea its abandoned orchard would become one of Willamette Valley's top Pinot Noir producers. In the early days of the pioneers, the site was a cattle ranch with a quarry. Today, the old barn is the only remnant of the time before the Willamette Valley became the king of New World Pinot Noir.

The property lies at the convergence of Willamette Valley's highest mountain range and the smallest AVA in Oregon, Ribbon Ridge. The shallow soils, which are rich in basalt, add a unique aspect to the terroir. Slow growing conditions allow for the gradual development of the texture and color compounds in the grape skins. As a result, the fruit has layers of intricate flavors, which translate into exciting, complex wines.

Ranked seventh on *Wine Spectator's* list of the top ten wines of the year in 2015, Colene Clemens Chehalem Mountain Dopp Creek Pinot Noir is a testament to Oregon's potential on the viticultural world stage. The winery's Margo Pinot Noir also placed on *Wine Spectator's* Top 100 wines of the year. The Adrian Pinot Noir, however, is the wine of

choice. Just like the Margo Pinot Noir, the Adrian is named after one of the owners' children. This Pinot is both elegant and rich, a complex product and a perfect example of Willamette Valley wine, which is some of the best in the world. When you visit Colene Clemens, sit on the patio with your vino in hand and enjoy a center-stage view of Willamette Valley's highest mountain, Bald Peak.

LAND MANAGER

Oregon Metro
38263 SW Dixon Mill Rd
Gaston, OR 97119
Phone: (503) 797-1545
www.oregonmetro.gov

WINERY

Colene Clemens
22501 NE Dopp Road
Newberg, OR 97132
Phone: (503) 662-4687
www.coleneclemens.com
Distance from trailhead: 8.9 miles

CAPE FALCON

VISIT A COASTAL OUTCROPPING THE SPANISH SAILED BY 250 YEARS AGO

STARTING POINT	DESTINATION
CAPE FALCON TRAILHEAD	CAPE FALCON
WINERY	**HIKE TYPE**
PUFFIN WINES	MODERATE
DOG FRIENDLY	**SEASON**
YES (ON LEASH)	YEAR-ROUND
FEES	**DURATION**
NONE	2 HOURS
MAP REFERENCE	**LENGTH**
POSTED AT TRAILHEAD	4.2 MILES
HIGHLIGHTS	**ELEVATION GAIN**
HAYSTACK ROCK	125 FEET

PINOT NOIR

WILLAMETTE VALLEY PINOT NOIR

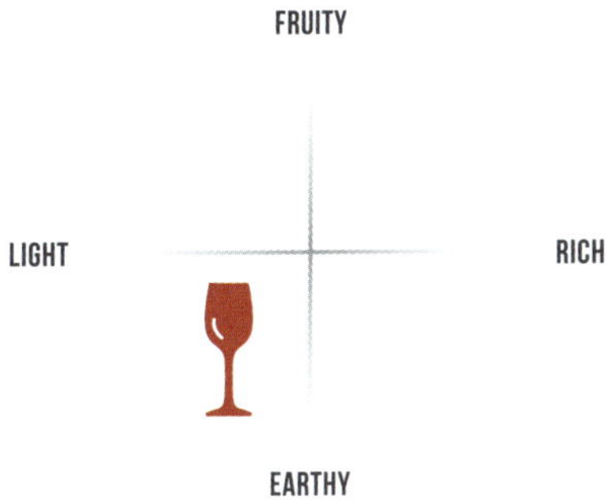

RED,
DRY,
STILL

RASBERRIES,
SPICE,
WET EARTH

RUBY

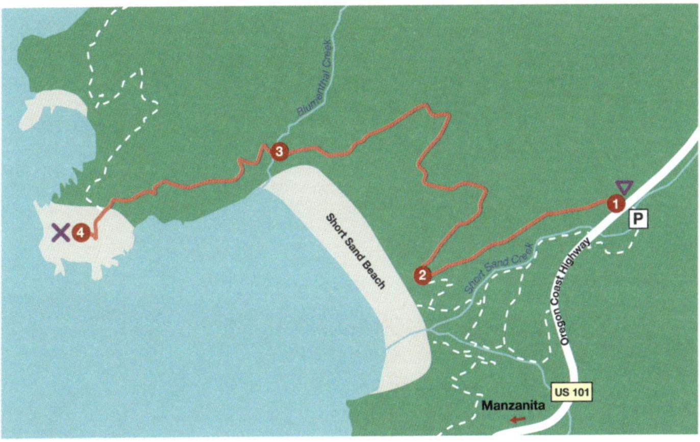

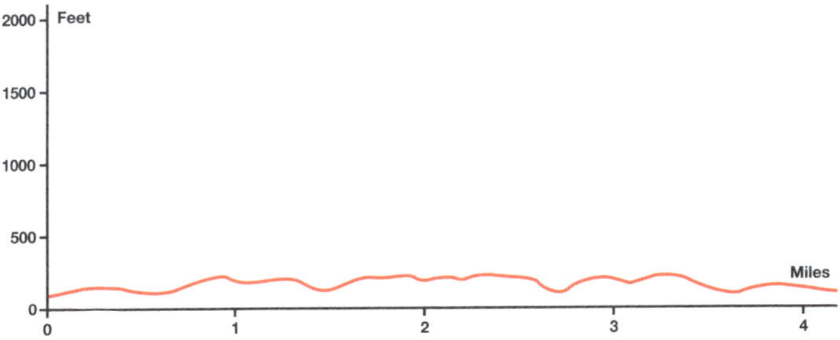

HIKE DESCRIPTION

Take a hike through history and enjoy wine tasting with Puffins on the Pacific coast.

Cannon Beach is a charming seaside village famous for its "Haystack Rock" and adorable tufted puffins. It owes its name to the USS Shark, a vessel used for ocean exploring and combating pirates in the West Indies and Africa. The ship met its demise one fateful day in 1846, not far from Cannon Beach. The town received its current name after a cannon from the shipwreck washed ashore. More cannons have been discovered in recent years, which has renewed interest in the origin story of the town's name.

The Cape Falcon Trail starts roughly 16 minutes away from Cannon Beach by car. The origin of the name "Falcon" has an Italian twist. On August 17th, 1775, the Spanish explorer Bruno de Hezeta was sailing along the misty waters of the Oregon Coast, roughly four miles from where Manzanita now lies. Hezeta bestowed the name "Sierra de Montefalco" on the cape, since August 17th was the day of Saint Clare of Montefalco, an Italian nun who died in 1308.

Wending through forests of saltwater-loving Sitka trees dressed in skirts of soft green moss, and featuring refreshing coastal views, the Cape Falcon Trail has all the elements of a perfect Oregon hike. Starting at the trailhead, you'll traverse a series of woodland areas, with several scenic views of the ocean coastline visible through the trees. At just over two miles, you'll arrive at the junction of the Arch Cape to Cape Falcon Trail. Heading left, our trail breaks out from the trees and delivers sweeping views of the Pacific Ocean. As you listen to the sound of the waves, imagine Spanish galleons sailing by as they did centuries ago.

TURN-BY-TURN DIRECTIONS

1. From the trailhead, proceed westward into the forest.
2. At 0.5 miles, reach the junction with the Kramer Memorial Trail and take the Cape Falcon Trail to the right.
3. At 1.5 miles, cross Blumenthal creek.
4. At 2.1 miles, reach the cape lookout and return the way you came.

FIND THE TRAILHEAD

Heading North from Manzanita, take US-101 North for 4.2 miles. The destination will be on the left (be prepared for a sharp turn). If taking US-101 South from Cannon Beach, travel 9.9 miles before turning right at the trailhead parking area.

THE WINE SHACK AND PUFFIN WINES

The Wine Shack has lived up to its motto, "Surprise and Delight," since its founding in 1977. Steven and Maryann Sinkler turned their dreams into reality after finding the shack for sale on craigslist in 2012. Voted "One of the Top Wine Stores in America" by *GQ* magazine, the Wine Shack offers an extensive selection of delightful wines from around the globe. This seaside shack does much more than sell Bordeaux and Napa Cabernet Sauvignon, however. The Shack crafts its own wine: Puffin Wines (yes, there's a puffin on the label). Sourcing fruit from across Oregon and working with several different winemakers, Steven Sinkler is able to produce a wide spectrum of bottlings for his Puffin label, ranging from Cabernet Sauvignon to Pinot Gris.

Heading up the Wine Shack's portfolio is the Puffin Pinot Noir. Awarded gold and platinum medals every year, Puffin Pinot Noir will remind you of being on Cannon Beach with the salty air filling your nose and a crisp and refreshing mist from crashing ocean waves on your skin. The Wine Shack and Puffin Pinot Noir will make for a memorable wine-tasting experience after a hike like this one along the Oregon Coast.

LAND MANAGER

Oregon Parks and Recreation Department
725 Summer Street NE, Suite C
Salem, OR 97301
Phone: (800) 551-6949
stateparks.oregon.gov

WINERY

The Wine Shack
124 N Hemlock Street
Cannon Beach, OR 97110
Phone: (503) 436-1100
www.thewineshack.wine
Distance from trailhead: 10.3 miles

THE COLUMBIA GORGE AND EASTERN OREGON

ANGEL'S REST

TAKE IN AN ANGEL'S VIEW OF THE COLUMBIA RIVER GORGE

STARTING POINT	DESTINATION
ANGEL'S REST TRAILHEAD	ANGEL'S REST BLUFF
WINERY	**HIKE TYPE**
EDGEFIELD	MODERATE
DOG FRIENDLY	**SEASON**
YES (LEASH REQUIRED)	YEAR-ROUND
FEES	**DURATION**
NONE	3 HOURS
MAP REFERENCE	**LENGTH**
AT TRAILHEAD	4.4 MILES (ROUND-TRIP)
HIGHLIGHTS	**ELEVATION GAIN**
VIEW OF GORGE	1,400 FEET

RED BLEND

BLACK RABBIT RED

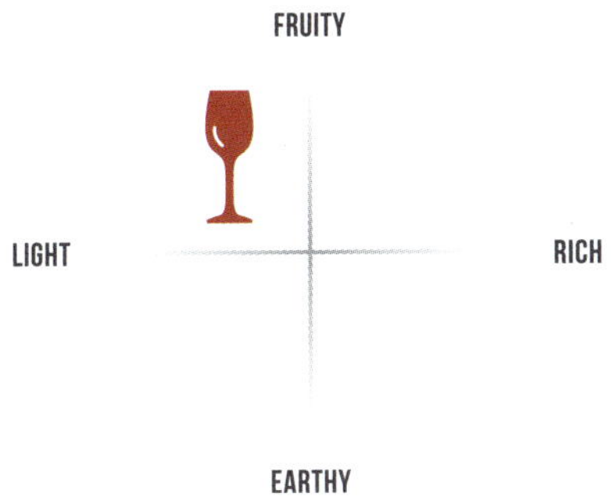

RED,
DRY,
STILL

CHERRIES,
BLUEBERRIES,
PLUM

RED

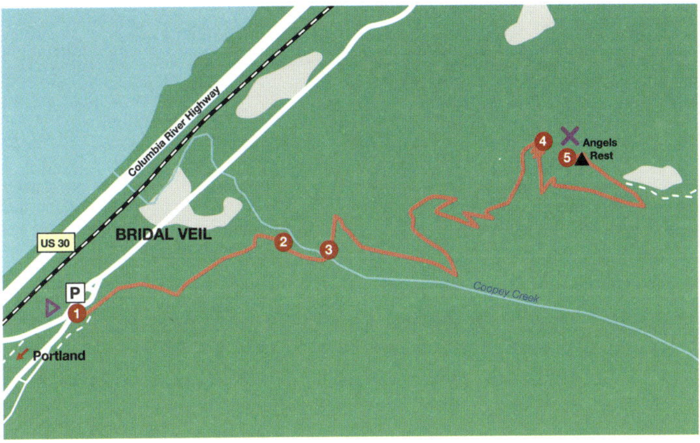

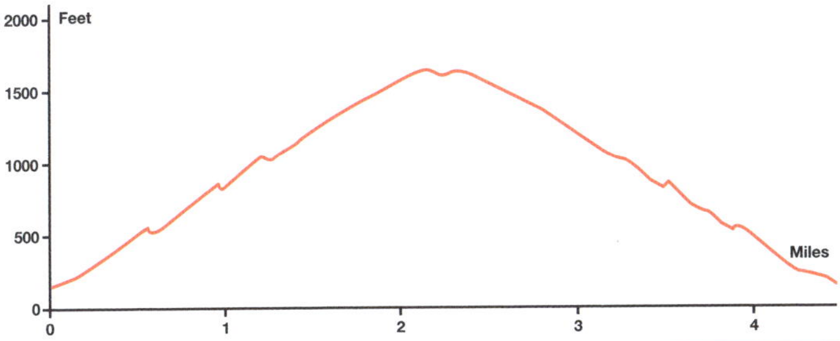

HIKE DESCRIPTION

Climb the heights above the Columbia River Gorge to find out why angels rest here; then step back in time and indulge in a glass of wine and a little nostalgia.

If you think the Columbia River Gorge is the perfect setting for a medieval fantasy film, you're not alone. This iconic canyon has appeared in several feature films, including the *Twilight* vampire series, *Bend of the River* with Jimmy Stewart, and the 1994 film *Maverick,* starring Mel Gibson and James Garner. While you won't spot cowboys, Native American tribes, or vampires here today, the Columbia River Gorge is ideal for an afternoon hike. Angel's Rest, located halfway between the Hood River and Portland, beckons you to climb the 1,500 feet to its summit, where you'll be rewarded with a good look at the awe-inspiring beauty of the mighty river.

Starting at the trailhead, you'll trek across a series of steep slopes with groves of maple trees and lush ferns. You'll reach the lower Coopey Falls viewpoint after about half a mile and then continue to the upper viewpoint, before finally crossing the Coopey Creek bridge. Here you'll notice charred and decaying timber from the Eagle Creek Fire of 2017. Despite the fire's visible destruction, the hike still boasts the beauty typical of the Pacific Northwest. After a couple of miles, you'll arrive at the Angel's Rest summit, which is covered with slabs of basalt stacked like stone tables. It's an idyllic place to get a bird's-eye perspective and panoramic photos of the dramatic gorge below.

TURN-BY-TURN DIRECTIONS

1. From the parking lot, follow the sign for the Angel's Rest Trail.
2. At 0.5 miles, reach the lower Coopey Falls viewpoint.
3. At 0.6 miles, reach the upper Coopey Falls viewpoint.
4. At 1.7 miles, come to a series of switchbacks.
5. At 2.2 miles, reach the Angel's Rest summit. Return the way you came.

FIND THE TRAILHEAD

From Portland, follow I-84 E to Bridal Veil. Take Exit 28 toward US-30/ Bridal Veil and follow it for 0.2 miles; then turn right toward the Historic Columbia River Highway. After 100 feet, turn right into the parking lot.

MCMENAMINS EDGEFIELD WINERY & TASTING ROOM

As famous for its tater tots as it is for craft beer, McMenamins is a hallmark of both Oregon and the Pacific Northwest. Founded by the McMenamins brothers, Mike and Brian, the family-owned operation became famous for founding the Mission Theater in 1987—the first theater pub in Oregon. Known for renovating a variety of historic buildings, the McMenamins chain has become a Swiss army knife of hospitality, food, and beverages. With over 50 locations in Washington and Oregon, McMenamins isn't your typical restaurant chain. And, as it runs distilleries, hotels, breweries, spas, and even a cigar pub, it's not surprising McMenamins also produces wine. Opened in 1990, the McMenamins Edgefield Winery sources fruit from across the Pacific Northwest, crafting a variety of red, white, sparkling, and rosé wines. Its most notable bottling, however, is the Black Rabbit Red Blend. While visiting the Edgefield Winery in eastern Portland, you'll have the opportunity to take in its ornate gardens, delightful vineyards, and spa. So, grab a delicious, juicy burger and a glass of Black Rabbit and enjoy the nostalgia (free of charge).

LAND MANAGER

Forest Service, USDA
902 Wasco Avenue, Suite 200
Hood River, OR 97031
Phone: (541) 308-1700
www.fs.usda.gov

WINERY

Edgefield Winery
2126 SW Halsey Street
Troutdale, OR 97060
Phone: (503) 665-2992
www.mcmenamins.com/edgefield
Distance from trailhead 12.9 miles

MULTNOMAH FALLS

HIKE THE SWITCHBACKS TO OREGON'S MOST ICONIC WATERFALL

PORTLAND

STARTING POINT	DESTINATION
MULTNOMAH TRAILHEAD PARK	MULTNOMAH FALLS
WINERY	**HIKE TYPE**
CATHEDRAL RIDGE	MODERATE
DOG FRIENDLY	**SEASON**
YES (LEASH REQUIRED)	YEAR-ROUND
FEES	**DURATION**
NONE	1 HOUR 30 MIN.
MAP REFERENCE	**LENGTH**
AT THE TRAILHEAD	2.4 MILES (ROUND-TRIP)
HIGHLIGHTS	**ELEVATION GAIN**
MULTNOMAH FALLS LODGE	788 FEET

RED BLEND

WINEMAKERS RESERVE

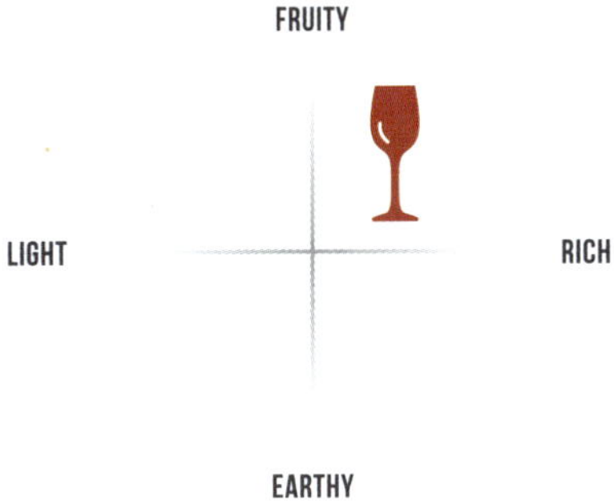

RED,
DRY,
STILL

SILKY,
JUICY,
RED FRUIT,
EARTH

GARNET

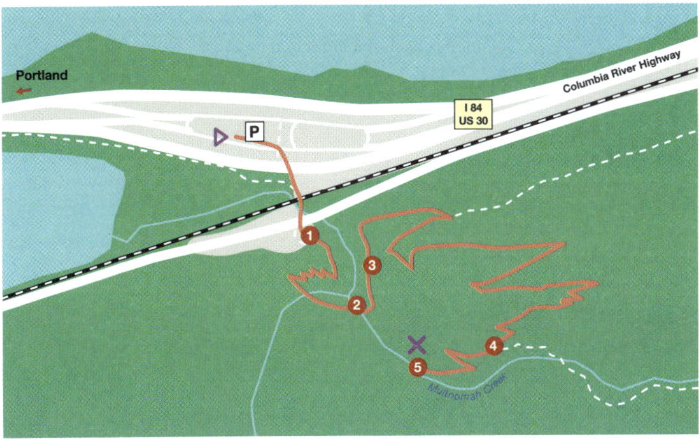

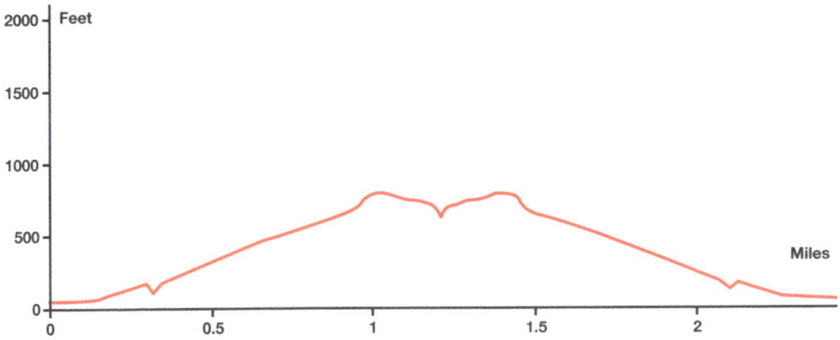

HIKE DESCRIPTION

Follow a switchback trail that ascends the cliffs of the Columbia Gorge for an unbeatable view of Upper Multnomah Falls. Then treat yourself to a tasting in the shadow of Mount Hood.

No Oregon hiking book would be complete without mentioning Multnomah Falls, the waterfall icon of Oregon. This stunning work of nature plunges a staggering 620 feet from basalt cliffs into the Columbia River Gorge, leaving close to two million visitors each year in awe of its beauty. The majestic landmark is located just 30 miles east of the cityscape of Portland, Oregon. Reminiscent of the plunging falls of Yosemite Valley, Multnomah Falls has a long and storied history among the local Multnomah tribe, and even Lewis and Clark wrote about seeing the Oregon waterfall icon on their 1805 expedition. According to oral traditions, the Multnomah tribe and waterfall are named after a powerful Native chief. While Chief Multnomah is considered a mythical figure by most contemporary historians, the oral lore of the local tribe brings the origin story of Multnomah Falls to life.

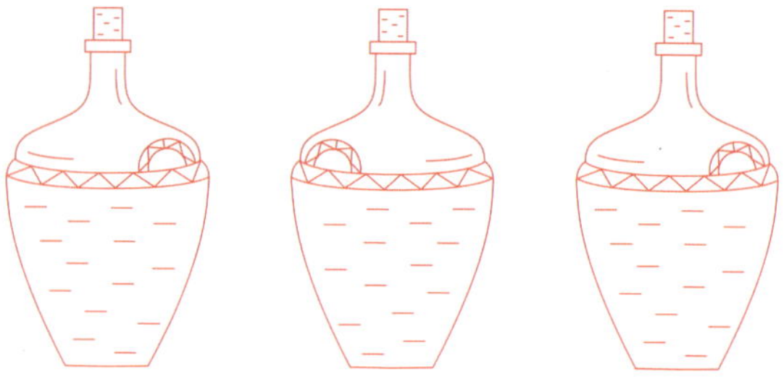

The first part of the two-tiered Multnomah Falls plummets 542 feet into a boulder-strewn pool; the second drops off for a further 69 feet. Between the two falls is the frequently photographed Benson Bridge. Just below the Benson Bridge lies Multnomah Lodge. Built in 1925, this historic landmark was constructed using every kind of rock and stone found along the Columbia Gorge. Inside, you'll find a gift shop, restaurant, and a coffee stand. Seeking a sugar rush? The lodge also sells fresh fudge!

You'll begin our trail at the base of Multnomah Falls and pass the historic lodge before trekking to the Benson Bridge. Crossing Benson Bridge, you'll see the rushing water plunging over the lower Multnomah Falls below your feet. From Benson Bridge, the trail ascends through a forest of fir, pine, and madrone trees as it winds along eleven switchbacks to the upper falls and views of the Columbia River and surrounding gorge. About a mile into the hike, you'll reach the end of the trail at a balcony overlooking Upper Multnomah Falls. If you are wary of heights, you should hang on tight as you watch Multnomah Creek freefall over the edge of the basalt cliff onto the pool of boulders below.

TURN-BY-TURN DIRECTIONS

1. From the Multnomah Lodge waterfall viewing area, follow the trailhead sign and proceed to the trailhead.
2. At 0.3 miles, arrive at Benson Bridge.
3. At 0.6 miles, arrive at the eleventh switchback and proceed to the top of the falls.
4. At 1.1 miles, reach the junction with the Larch Mountain Trail and the Wahkeena Falls Trail. Continue straight, following the sign for "Top of Falls" (Trail 441A).
5. At 1.2 miles, reach the Upper Multnomah Falls viewpoint. Return the way you came.

FIND THE TRAILHEAD

From Portland, take I-84 East. After 28 miles, take Exit 31 (on the left) toward the Multnomah Falls parking area. Take the same exit if you're traveling west toward Portland. If you want to avoid traffic issues, there is transportation to and from the falls operated by the Columbia Area Transit system. The schedule is available on their website at www.ride-catbus.org.

CATHEDRAL RIDGE

After purchasing Flerchinger Vineyards from his neighbor in 2003, Robb Bell changed its name to Cathedral Ridge Winery, a reference to a majestic dagger ridge that leads to the summit of Mount Hood. The winery gained attention early on, earning the 2007 Oregon Winery of the Year award from *Wine Press Northwest* magazine. Today, the winery remains a notable producer not just in the region but in the whole of the Pacific Northwest. The head winemaker and Sonoma County winemaking star, Michael Sebastiani of the Sebastiani winemaking family, directs the Cathedral Ridge team in producing dozens of distinctive award-winning wines. The juicy Zinfandel, delicate Pinot Noir and Chardonnay, spicy Syrah, Grenache, and even Barbera ensure that everyone will find a wine to their liking among Cathedral Ridge's bottlings. The winery's flagship wine is the Winemaker's Reserve Cuvee, consisting of the classic Bordeaux grape varieties Cabernet Sauvignon, Cabernet Franc, Merlot, Malbec, and Petite Verdot. This wine merges the best qualities of each grape and brings them together to produce richness, depth, and elegance.

LAND MANAGER

Columbia River Gorge National Scenic Area Office
902 Wasco Avenue
Suite 200 Hood River, OR 97031
Phone: (541) 308-1700
www.fs.usda.gov

WINERY

Cathedral Ridge
4200 Post Canyon Dr
Hood River, OR 97031
Phone: (541) 386-2882
www.cathedralridgewinery.com
Distance from trailhead: 32 miles

WAHKEENA FALLS

A SHORT HIKE TO TWO STUNNING WATERFALLS

STARTING POINT	DESTINATION
WAKHENNA FALLS TRAILHEAD #420	FAIRY FALLS
WINERY	HIKE TYPE
GORGE WHITE HOUSE	EASY
DOG FRIENDLY	SEASON
YES (LEASH REQUIRED)	YEAR-ROUND
FEES	DURATION
YES	1 HOUR
MAP REFERENCE	LENGTH
AT TRAILHEAD	2 MILES (ROUND-TRIP)
HIGHLIGHTS	ELEVATION GAIN
HISTORIC COLUMBIA RIVER HIGHWAY	820 FEET

ROSÉ

COLUMBIA GORGE ROSÉ

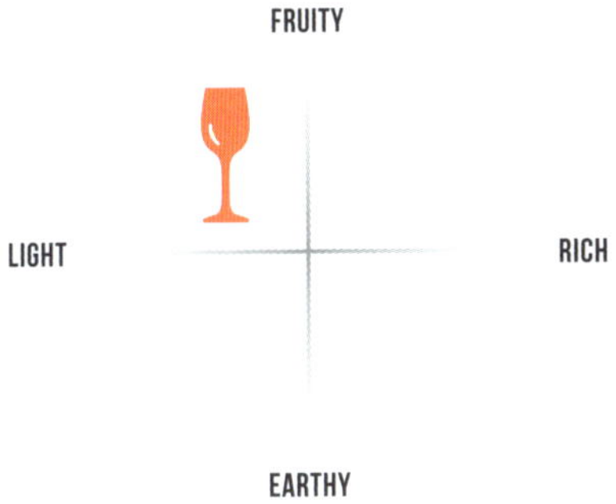

ROSÉ, OFF-DRY, STILL

FLORAL, STRAWBERRY, WATERMELON

LIGHT PINK

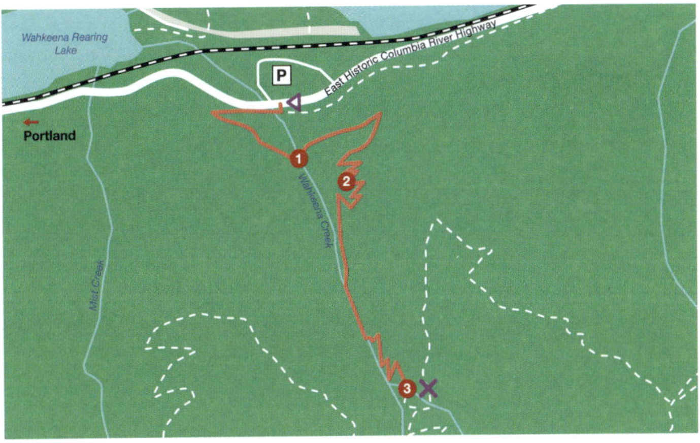

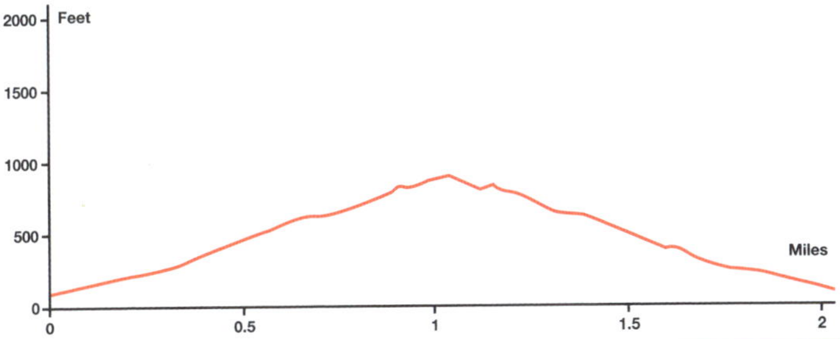

HIKE DESCRIPTION

View two magical waterfalls and then gorge yourself on a slice of paradise.

With roughly 90 waterfalls running along the Columbia Gorge, the area from Portland to Hood River is known as Waterfall Alley. It can be difficult to pick just one to hike when visiting the gorge. Although the Multnomah Falls are often considered the most stunning, the Wahkeena Falls, a 242-foot natural wonder, are not to be dismissed. "Wahkeena" means "Most Beautiful" in the Yakima language.

With this hike, you'll hit two birds with one stone: about a mile in, you'll get a look at "Fairy Falls," which are smaller than Wahkeena, but just as beautiful. Rather than plunging down in free-fall, this waterfall washes over a moss-clad rock face. It was originally named "Ghost Falls," because when the sun hits it just right, the falls glow as if there is a spirit in them. If you're looking for an extended waterfall hiking adventure, the Wahkeena Falls Trail #420 also connects with the Devil's Rest (See Angel's Rest Chapter), the Vista Point Trail #419, and the Multnomah Falls Trail. This combination would make for an approximately five-mile trek if you hiked to the Wahkeena Falls spring and the Wiesendanger and Ecola Falls.

TURN-BY-TURN DIRECTIONS

1. From the parking lot, proceed up Trail #420 for 0.2 miles and reach Wahkeena Falls. After appreciating the falls, continue on Trail #420.
2. At 0.7 miles, arrive at Lemmons Viewpoint area. Continue on Trail #420.
3. At 1.0 miles, arrive at Fairy Falls. Return the way you came.

FIND THE TRAILHEAD

From Troutdale, follow I-84 East for 10 miles and take Exit 31. Proceed on Bridal Veil Road for 0.2 miles before continuing onto the Historic Columbia River Highway for an additional 2.5 miles. The Wahkeena Falls Day-Use Area and Trailhead will be on the left.

GORGE WHITE HOUSE

In 1910, Iowa farmer Martin Michael set out to build the "finest house in the [Columbia] valley" for his wealthy midwestern wife. The Gorge White House attracts visitors year-round with its architectural charm and its delicious food and drinks. The Colonial Dutch Revival house, with its fluted porch columns and distinctively German-style gambrel roof, will transport you back in time. Purchased by the Kennedy family in 2012, the small farm and orchard surrounding it is a slice of paradise. The family chef, Jack Kennedy, an alumnus of Cordon Bleu in France and Australia, contributes his culinary expertise to the mouth-watering cuisine at the family food truck, which produces a plethora of savory sandwiches, burgers, and flatbreads. It's difficult not to purchase everything on the menu, which includes pear quesadillas with melted goat cheese and bacon, flatbreads topped with blueberry sausage and mozzarella cheese, and a classic burger made from locally sourced beef and topped with buns that are baked fresh daily.

While the food truck is sure to excite your taste buds, the team at the Gorge White House also produces their own wine and cider! Working with a Négociant-Éleveur, (someone who acquires grapes and makes

wine for people) the Gorge White House offers several reds, including Cabernet Sauvignon, Pinot Noir, and a Red Blend. It also makes Chardonnay, Riesling, Pinot Gris, and even a distinct pear wine crafted from fruit grown on the Kennedy family farm. But it is the rosé, made from the juicy Italian Dolcetto grape and blended with small amounts of spicy Tempranillo, that is the wine of choice. Fermented at low temperatures in stainless steel, the wine retains its more delicate aromas. Leading with notes of strawberry, raspberry, and cherries, and followed by a touch of sweetness, this rosé will cut through the summer heat and refresh your spirits after a hike in the Mount Hood Forest.

LAND MANAGER

Columbia River Gorge National Scenic Area Office
902 Wasco Avenue
Suite 200 Hood River, OR 97031
Phone: (541) 308-1700
www.fs.usda.gov

WINERY

Gorge White House and Cellars
2265 OR-35
Hood River, OR 97031
Phone: (541) 386-2828
www.thegorgewhitehouse.com
Distance from trailhead: 38.0 miles

PUNCH BOWL FALLS

HIKE UP A SERIES OF CRAGS TO A CHARMING WATERFALL

COLUMBIA GORGE

STARTING POINT	DESTINATION
EAGLE CREEK TRAILHEAD	TUNNEL FALLS
WINERY	HIKE TYPE
MOUNT HOOD WINERY	STRENUOUS
DOG FRIENDLY	SEASON
YES (LEASH REQUIRED)	YEAR-ROUND
FEES	DURATION
YES ($5 DAY-USE FEE)	1.5 HOURS
MAP REFERENCE	LENGTH
POSTED AT TRAILHEAD	11.8 MILES (ROUND-TRIP)
HIGHLIGHTS	ELEVATION GAIN
TUNNEL FALLS	1,046 FEET

RIESLING

ESTATE RIESLING

FRUITY

LIGHT

RICH

EARTHY

WHITE, STILL, OFF-DRY

PEAR, HONEYSUCKLE

WHITE

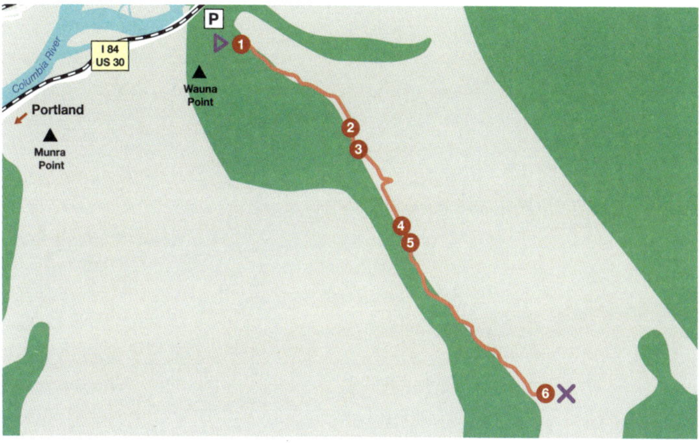

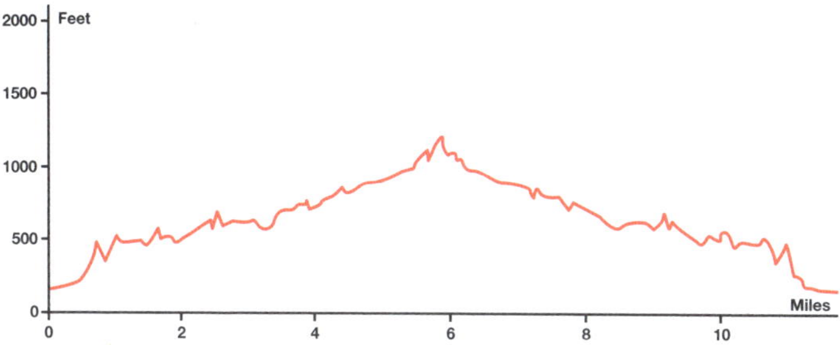

HIKE DESCRIPTION

Explore towering waterfalls and rumbling mountain streams on a dramatic hike. Finish your day sipping on a sweet Riesling paired with even sweeter views of the mighty Mount Hood.

Punch Bowl Falls (three words) should not be confused with Punchbowl Falls (two words), which is located further upriver. To get to Punch Bowl Falls, you'll follow Eagle Creek, a tributary of the Columbia River that features a number of spectacular waterfalls as it winds through dramatic ravines, canyon ledges, and expansive alpine forests. Since the devastation of the Eagle Creek fire of 2017, much of the area's former beauty has returned, with new growth among the old trees including purple and pink fireweed flowers.

For this hike, you'll need to purchase a $5.00 parking pass at the visitor center and trailhead. The trail begins on the northeastern edge of Eagle Creek, near the Columbia River. Staying on the eastern flank of Eagle Creek, you'll begin a steady ascent above the canyon. As you climb up the ravine, the sound of rushing water will slowly fade. The path consists primarily of shelf-like trails cut out of the cliff. The park service has installed cables to hold onto as you walk.

Listen carefully, as you might well hear the scream of an eagle while making your way up the creek. And you'll hear the gushing torrent of water from Punch Bowl Falls long before you see it. A heavy flow of roaring water plunges into a bubbling blue crystalline bowl-shaped pool. Several other waterfalls lie further up the trail, including the famous Tunnel Falls. The hike to Tunnel Falls is considerably longer (roughly 12 miles round-trip), but it's well worth it if you're feeling energetic. If you opt for the longer route, don't miss the rock tunnel carved out right behind the waterfall!

TURN-BY-TURN DIRECTIONS

1. From the trailhead, proceed toward Lower Punch Bowl Falls.
2. At 1.8 miles, reach Lower Punch Bowl Falls.
3. At 2.0 miles, arrive at the Upper Punch Bowl Falls viewpoint. From here, either head back the way you came, or, if you're up for a longer hike, continue as described below.
4. At 3.2 miles, reach the Loowit Falls viewpoint.
5. At 3.3 miles, cross High Bridge.
6. At 5.9 miles, arrive at Tunnel Falls. Return the way you came.

FIND THE TRAILHEAD

From Portland, merge onto I-84 East/US-30 East and follow it for 32.6 miles. Take Exit 41 and proceed for 0.6 miles. Turn right onto NE Eagle Creek Lane and continue for 0.5 miles to the end of the road and the parking lot and trailhead.

MOUNT HOOD WINERY

Hood River may be the world leader in Anjou pear production, but this quaint riverside town has also earned itself a solid reputation for crafting quality wine. Brothers Steve and Don Bickford used to grow fruit trees on their land. Then, in 2000, the Bickford family took up an expensive hobby—winegrowing. Steve hired former high-school classmate Rich Cushman to lead the winemaking operations, which led to Mount Hood being named the 2016 Oregon Winery of the Year by *Wine Press Northwest* magazine. Mount Hood Winery produces a diverse selection of crisp whites, delicate rosés, and firm but silky reds—as well as a unique pear wine for those looking to try something different. Rich Cushman studied his craft in Germany and has an affinity for Riesling, the hallmark German grape. Crafted in an off-dry style, the Estate Riesling has the slightest trace of sweetness, which makes a lovely contrast to the winery's equally delicious Dry Riesling. It is an enchanting experience to sip fine wine on the patio, with Mount Hood's snow-capped peak as a magnificent backdrop; the setting is reminiscent of a Tolkien novel. Don't be surprised if a hobbit, a dozen dwarves, and a wizard begin tasting wine alongside you at the tasting room.

Riesling: Considered the flagship of German wines, Riesling is one of the most versatile wine grapes in the world. Ranging from dry to intensely sweet, it can express a variety of personalities, depending on where it is grown. The most sought-after quality of the grape (particularly of aged Rieslings) is its iconic "petrol aroma." Quite literally, the wine will display aromas of petrol, kerosene, or rubber tires. This flavor is due to relatively high concentrations of TDN, a naturally occurring compound in the grape, and might be more or less intense depending on the region and the

winemaker. Many people might turn their noses up at the idea of a fossil-fuel-scented wine, but rest assured that the aroma can be delightful when integrated well. Like Gruner Veltliner, Riesling can age for decades without tiring, a rare quality for white wines but one that makes them perfect for collectors.

LAND MANAGER

Columbia River Gorge National Scenic Area Office
902 Wasco Avenue Suite 200
Hood River, OR 97031
Phone: (541) 308-1700
www.fs.usda.gov

WINERY

Mount Hood Winery
2882 Van Horn Drive
Hood River, OR 97031
Phone: (541) 386-8333
http://mthoodwinery.com/
Distance from trailhead: 30.9 miles

TAMANAWAS FALLS

AN ENCOUNTER WITH A FRIENDLY GUARDIAN SPIRIT

STARTING POINT	DESTINATION
TAMANAWAS FALLS TRAILHEAD	TAMANAWAS FALLS
WINERY	**HIKE TYPE**
STAVE AND STONE	MODERATE
DOG FRIENDLY	**SEASON**
YES (LEASH REQUIRED)	LATE SPRING–FALL
FEES	**DURATION**
YES ($5.00 DAY PASS)	3 HOURS
MAP REFERENCE	**LENGTH**
POSTED AT TRAILHEAD	3.4 MILES (ROUND-TRIP)
HIGHLIGHTS	**ELEVATION GAIN**
HOOD RIVER LAVENDER FARM	580 FEET

BROKEN BOULDER PINOT NOIR BLANC

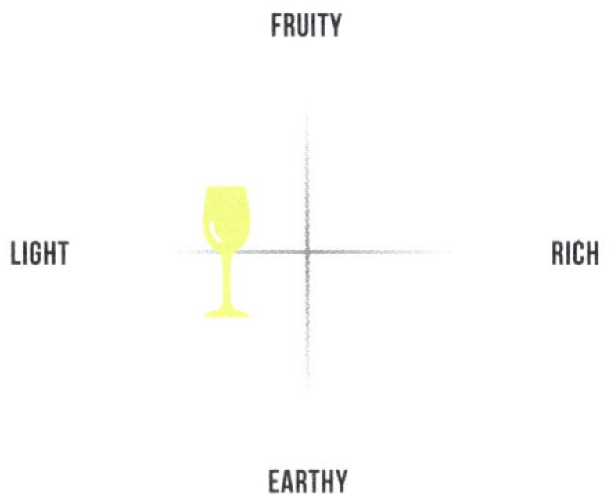

WHITE,
DRY,
STILL

APRICOT,
NECTARINE,
MELON

PALE, STRAW

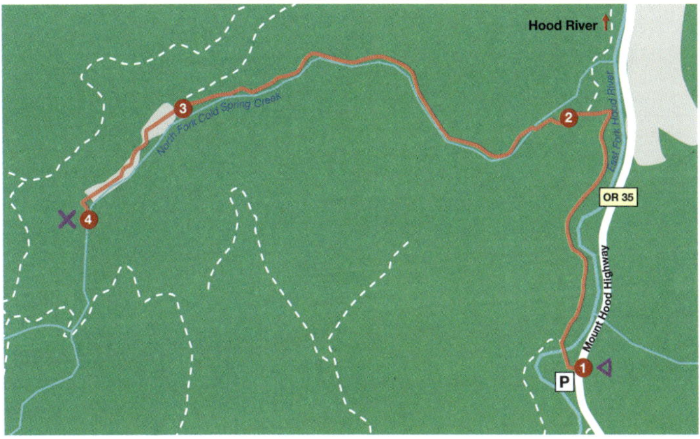

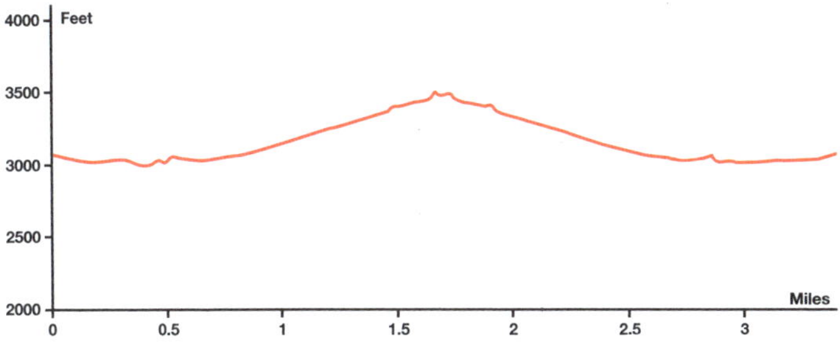

HIKE DESCRIPTION

Meet the guardian spirit of a Tamawanas waterfall. Then sip vino in a wine garden while enjoying views of Mt. Adams.

Tamawanas means "friendly guardian spirit" in Chinook, and you'll understand the name when you encounter the silky veil of water plunging from a concave basalt cliff into a bubbling stream at Tamawanas Falls. This hike is popular (for good reason) and can become crowded on summer weekends. I recommend you visit midweek and in the morning. Starting at the trailhead just off Highway 35, you'll begin the journey to the friendly guardian spirit by hiking along Cold Spring Creek. The sweet chime of running water creates a relaxing ambiance as you trek through thick forests of hemlock, cedar, and mighty Douglas fir. After about half a mile, you'll bear left and cross a single-log footbridge to the other side of Cold Spring Creek; this marks the beginning of the Tamanawas Falls Trail. As you move deeper into the conifer woodland, you may occasionally spy columbines, twin flowers, and clusters of bunchberries. Soon, you'll begin to hear the falls. As you approach, the sound of Cold Spring Creek will be drowned out by the trembling roar of the Tamanawas waterfall. The 100-foot falls douse moss-clad rocks and visitors alike with their mist, a refreshing conclusion to a delightful woodland adventure.

TURN-BY-TURN DIRECTIONS

1. From the parking lot off Highway 35, begin walking on the East Fork Trail #650.
2. At 0.6 miles, stay left and cross the log footbridge. Continue on the Tamanawas Falls Trail #650A.
3. At 1.4 miles, reach the junction with the Elk Meadows Trail. Stay left on the Tamanawas Falls Trail.
4. At 1.7 miles, arrive at the waterfall. Return the way you came.

FIND THE TRAILHEAD

From Hood River, take Highway 35 South towards Mount Hood. At milepost 72 (roughly 0.25 miles from the Sherwood Campground), turn right into the parking area at the sign for the Tamanawas Falls trailhead.

STAVE AND STONE (WINERY AT THE VINEYARD)

"Stave" is the both the owner's last name and a word for the wood from which a bow is made, while "Stone" refers to the giant basalt boulders that once littered the parcel of land where this vineyard is now situated. The ancient volcanic landscape of the Hood River area is an ideal place to taste delicious cheese, salami, and refreshing wine while enjoying views of the picturesque orchards and the distant Mount Adams. The winery has a primary tasting room and patio, but don't forget to check out its wine garden and pavilion. Here you can avoid the bustle of the tasting room, purchase wine by the bottle, and sip vino on the lawn area in full view of the mountains. The Stave and Stone Vineyards are the perfect place to stop after a hike, and they'll seem even more perfect as soon as you're sipping a Pinot Noir Blanc. Juicy and floral, this wine leads with notes of nectarine and peach, closely followed by savory apricot and lemon, all of which are laced together by a bright thread of racing acidity. Note that reservations are required at Stave and Stone.

Be sure you also make time to stop by the Hood River Lavender Farms (partly owned by the Stave and Stone family), which are known for crafting anything and everything made from lavender. From soaps,

oils, and candles to culinary products like lavender-infused chocolates and even tea, the Hood River Lavender Farms are a destination in and of themselves.

Pinot Noir Blanc: Not to be confused with Pinot Blanc, Pinot Noir Blanc actually comes from Pinot Noir grapes pressed quickly after picking to avoid color extraction from the skins. The end product is a clean but refreshing white wine ideal for pairing with savory seafood and spicy Asian cuisine.

LAND MANAGER

Forest Headquarters
16400 Champion Way
Sandy, OR 97055
Phone: (503) 668-1700
www.fs.usda.gov

WINERY

Stave and Stone Vineyards
3827 Fletcher Dr
Hood River, OR 97031
Phone: (541) 490-9461
www.staveandstone.com
Distance from trailhead: 16.9 miles

TWIN TUNNELS

HIKE THROUGH HISTORY TO OREGON'S "AXENSTRASSE"

STARTING POINT	DESTINATION
MARK HATFIELD WEST TRAILHEAD	TWIN TUNNELS
WINERY	HIKE TYPE
WY'EAST VINEYARDS	EASY
DOG FRIENDLY	SEASON
YES (LEASH REQUIRED)	YEAR-ROUND
FEES	DURATION
YES ($5.00 DAY-USE FEE)	1.5 HOURS
MAP REFERENCE	LENGTH
POSTED AT TRAILHEAD	3.7 MILES (ROUND-TRIP)
HIGHLIGHTS	ELEVATION GAIN
ENGRAVINGS ON THE WALLS OF THE TWIN TUNNELS	400 FEET

PINOT NOIR

BLUE CHIP PINOT NOIR

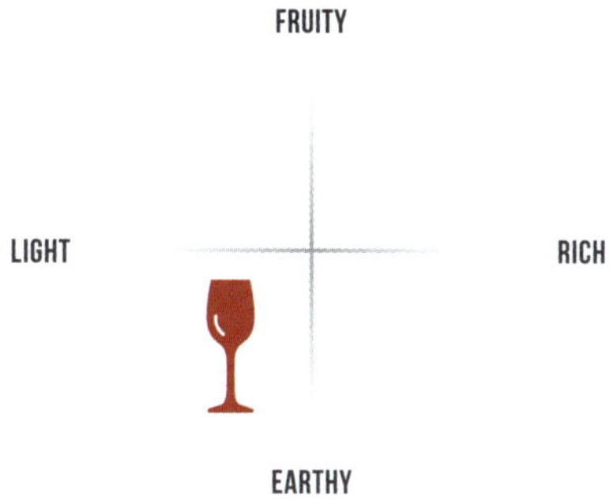

RED,
DRY,
STILL

EARTHY,
TART RASPBERRIES,
SWEET CHERRIES

PALE RUBY

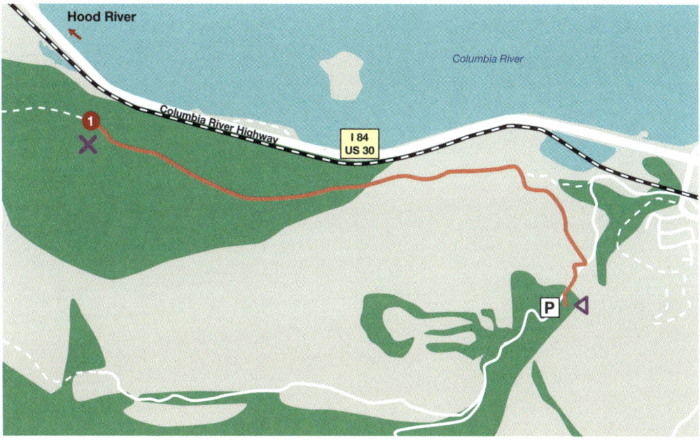

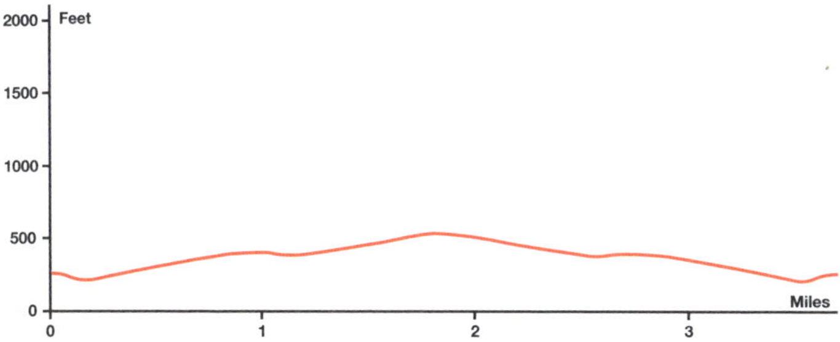

HIKE DESCRIPTION

Tunnel your way to great views and then enjoy a sip of wine at an eclectic vineyard.

The Mosier Twin Tunnels walk takes hikers between Hood River and Mosier, offering up-close views of the Columbia River and a walk through history. Part of the original Columbia River Highway, the tunnels were constructed to provide access to higher points of the gorge. However, after numerous landslides, they fell into disrepair and were finally abandoned in the 1950s. After extensive renovation, they were reopened to the public in 2000 as part of a hiking and biking path. Like Switzerland's famous Axenstrasse, the tunnels are not completely enclosed; looking though the arched openings, you'll see the river below, and while inside them, you'll have enough light to see the hundred-year-old wall engravings left by hunters who took shelter in the tunnels during a snowstorm.

The trail rises and dips along the Oregon side of the gorge, providing spectacular views of towering cliffs, decorative rock columns, and jagged ledges. Partway down the trail, you'll spy Eighteen Mile Island. This secluded piece of land once belonged to an Ohio railway conductor who moved to the gorge area and was said to have turned chicken farmer. Old maps call it "Chicken Charlie's Island." While Charlie was probably not a chicken farmer, the island's name certainly makes it more memorable. The island is even briefly mentioned by Lewis and Clark in their account of their journey to the Pacific Ocean. You can reach the tunnels from the West Trailhead (7.0 miles round-trip), but we'll start at the East Trailhead (2.1 miles round-trip).

TURN-BY-TURN DIRECTIONS

1. From the trailhead, take the Mark O. Hatfield East Trail (pavement) for 1.8 miles to reach the Twin Tunnels (and Chicken Charlie's Island viewpoint). Return the way you came.

FIND THE TRAILHEAD

Traveling East on Sherman Avenue in Hood River, turn left onto 13th Street. Proceed for 100 feet and then turn right onto State Street. Proceed for 1.1 miles and then take a slight left onto Old Columbia River Drive/Old US Highway 30. Continue for 1.3 miles and then turn left into the parking lot marked by the trailhead sign.

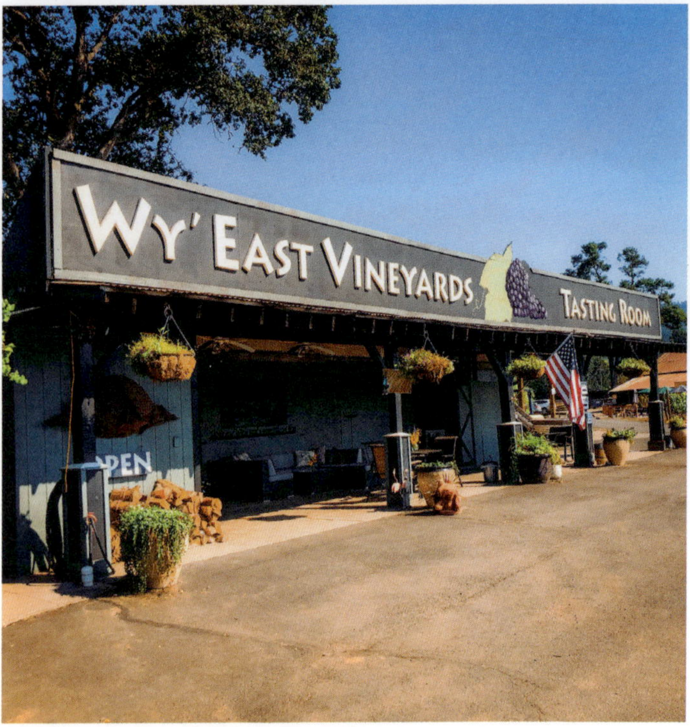

WY'EAST VINEYARDS

Founded by a former Michigan farmer, Wy'East Vineyards is the perfect example of why you shouldn't judge a book by its cover. Though its tasting room is nothing more than a converted fruit stand, Wy'East crafts wines equal to those of any fine establishment. It's bottlings range from refreshing whites to crunchy, juicy, and savory reds. Wy'East is the original native name for Mount Hood; in folklore, Wy'East is a spirit that fights the spirit of Mount Adams for a fair maiden, Mount Saint Helens. On weekends, Wy'East operates a seasonal food truck with perfect post-hike food. There is also a bocce pit you might enjoy bowling a round in. The quirky Easter Island head near the vineyard adds to Wy'East's eclectic chracter. Its featured bottling is the Blue Chip Pinot Noir, which is made in the "whole cluster" style (see the Silver Falls Canyon chapter for more about whole cluster wines). Wy'East's method of fermenting the grapes with the stems results in an earthy Pinot Noir encased by delicate fruit flavors of raspberry, maraschino cherry, and spice—all threaded together by a silky but sturdy texture.

LAND MANAGER

Oregon Parks and Recreation Department
725 Summer Street NE, Suite C
Salem, OR 97301
Phone: (800) 551-6949
www.oregon.gov

WINERY

Wy'East Vineyards
3189 OR-35
Hood River, OR 97031
Phone: (541) 386-1277
www.wyeastvineyards.com
Distance from trailhead: 6.7 miles

TOM MCCALL POINT TRAIL

"DON'T COME HERE TO LIVE!"

STARTING POINT	DESTINATION
ROWENA CREST VIEWPOINT	TOM MCCALL POINT
WINERY	HIKE TYPE
MARCHESI VINEYARDS	MODERATE
DOG FRIENDLY	SEASON
NO	MARCH–OCTOBER
FEES	DURATION
NONE	3 HOURS
MAP REFERENCE	LENGTH
POSTED AT TRAILHEAD	3.2 MILES (ROUND-TRIP)
HIGHLIGHTS	ELEVATION GAIN
MOUNT HOOD	920 FEET

BARBERA

COLUMBIA VALLEY BARBERA

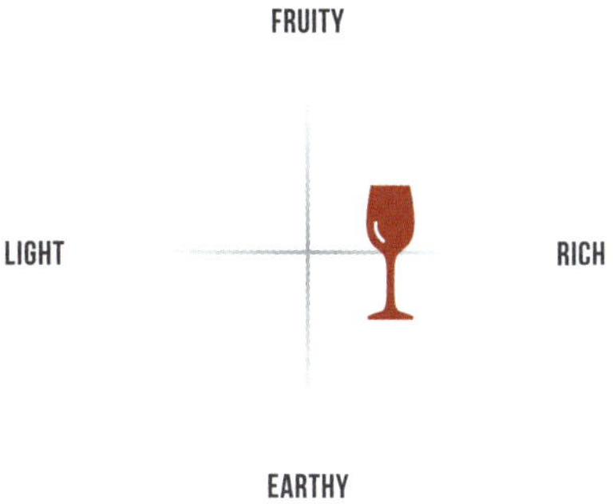

RED,
DRY,
STILL

SPICE,
CHERRY,
ZIPPY ACID

RED

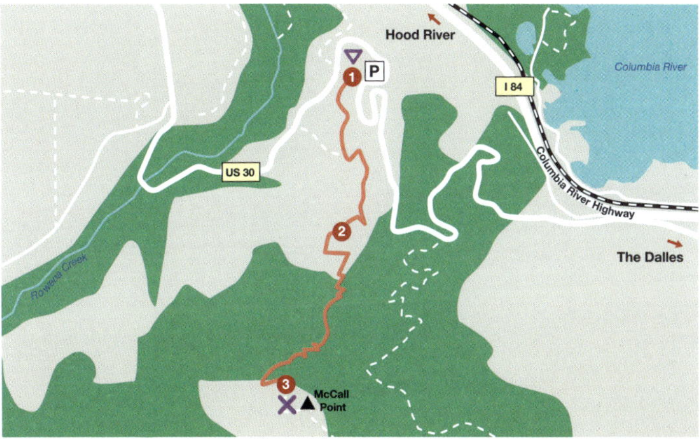

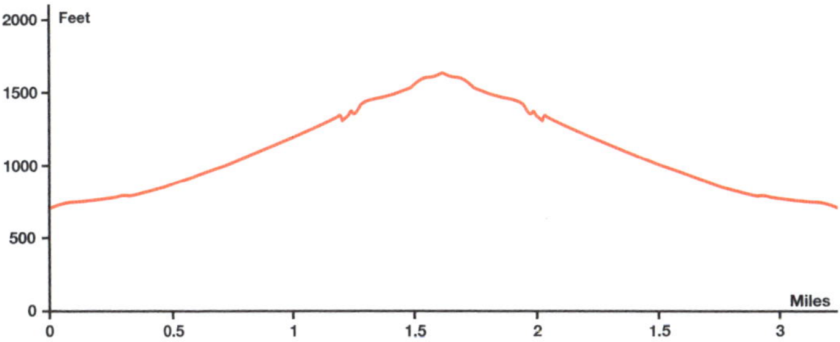

HIKE DESCRIPTION

Stop and smell the wildflowers (hundreds of different kinds!). Post-hike, enjoy an Italian wine tasting experience on Oregon's Hood River.

Former Oregon governor Tom McCall once said, "Come visit us again and again. This is a state of excitement. But, for heaven's sake, don't come here to live." The Tom McCall Point Trail is certainly well worth a visit. It passes through the Tom McCall preserve, 231 acres of wildflower heaven with over 300 species of unique plant life. Sprinkled across swelling grasslands, these wildflowers add exuberant color to the landscape. You might see Indian paintbrush, purple lupine, and the pinkish grass widow. The preserve is open from March to October.

The trail begins at the Rowena Crest Viewpoint, which offers dramatic views of the Columbia Gorge. Follow the trail as it traverses through expansive meadows (if you visit in May, they'll be full of bright yellow balsamroot). Soon the trail begins a steeper ascent continuing through groves of arching oak and thickets of brush. You'll catch glimpses of Mount Hood as you climb upward. At about 1,700 feet, Tom McCall Point offers stunning views of Mount Hood and Mount Adams, the iconic centerpieces of the Columbia River Gorge landscape.

TURN-BY-TURN DIRECTIONS

1. Begin at Rowena Crest Viewpoint and follow the signs for the Tom McCall Point Trail.
2. At 0.7 miles, reach the first switchback. (The second and third switchbacks occur at 1.2 and 1.5 miles.)
3. At 1.6 miles, reach the Tom McCall Point summit. Return the way you came.

FIND THE TRAILHEAD

From I-84 E, take Exit 69 onto US-30 Historic Columbia River Highway toward Mosier. Continue for 6.6 miles. The Rowena Crest Viewpoint and parking lot are on the right.

From I-84 W, take Exit 76 to Rowena. Turn left onto US-30 Historic Columbia River Highway. Turn right at the signs for the Historic Columbia River Highway Westward. Travel 2.6 miles until you reach the Rowena Crest Viewpoint and parking lot on your left.

MARCHESI VINEYARD AND WINERY

It will come as no surprise that this winery has Italian roots. Born in Borgosesia, Piedmont, Franco Marchesi traveled to the USA at age 22 and became a sommelier. He started out working aboard cruise ships and in high-end restaurants. When he first visited Hood River, it reminded him of his home in Italy. He purchased an abandoned orchard, where he planted grapes and made wine like his grandfather. Marchesi Winery has gone from a few humble vines to one of the most notable destinations in Hood River wine country. Prosciutto with cheese, Prosecco and crackers—you won't know whether you're in Piedmont or Hood River, as the tasting experience is strictly Italian. There's a chance you might even encounter the passionate Franco Marchesi himself. Marchesi imports authentic Italian Prosecco for his guests, but his estate production of over a dozen wines is just as noteworthy as the foreign bubbly. If Grenache is the big brother of Pinot Noir, Barbera is its Italian cousin: it's bright, lively, and expressive. Marchesi's Barbera is a classic Oregon wine instilled with the spirit of Italy. Enjoy a tasting on the back patio in the crisp alpine air, surrounded by grapevines, cheerful conversation, and world-class wine.

Barbera: This northern Italian grape produces juicy and refreshing wines with soft tannins and deep red berry flavors. While it's grown throughout Italy, the best-known examples come from Piedmont's Barbera d'Asti DOCG (a particular growing area). The naturally high acidity of Barbera makes it an ideal pairing partner for a variety of cuisines.

LAND MANAGER

The Nature Conservatory
821 SE 14th Avenue
Portland, OR 97214
Phone: (503) 802-8100
www.nature.org

WINERY

Marchesi Vineyards
3955 Belmont Drive
Hood River, OR 97031
Phone: (541) 386-1800
www.marchesivineyards.com
Distance from trailhead: 16.5 miles

SOUTH FORK WALLA WALLA

"A DAMN FOOL DOCTOR WITH MORE MONEY THAN BRAINS"

STARTING POINT	DESTINATION
HARRIS PARK TRAILHEAD	SOUTH FORK RIVER MOUTAIN RAVINE
WINERY	HIKE TYPE
ZERBA CELLARS	MODERATE
DOG FRIENDLY	SEASON
YES	YEAR-ROUND
FEES	DURATION
NONE	2 HOURS
MAP REFERENCE	LENGTH
AT TRAILHEAD	4.2 MILES (ROUND-TRIP)
HIGHLIGHTS	ELEVATION GAIN
HISTORIC DOWNTOWN WALLA WALLA	234 FEET

SYRAH

ROCKS SYRAH

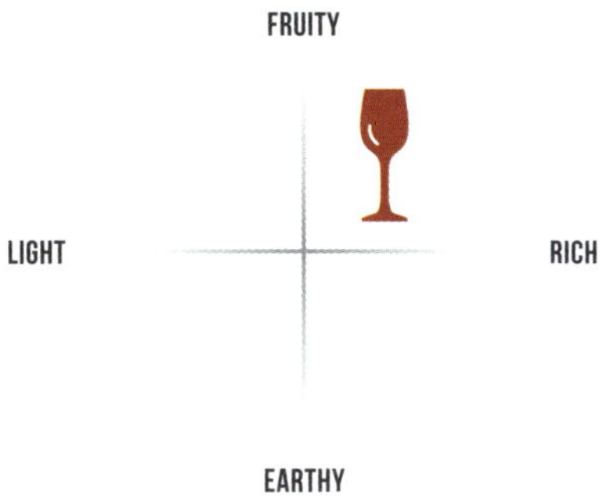

RED,
DRY,
STILL

JUICY,
RICH,
TOASTY,
GAMEY

GARNET

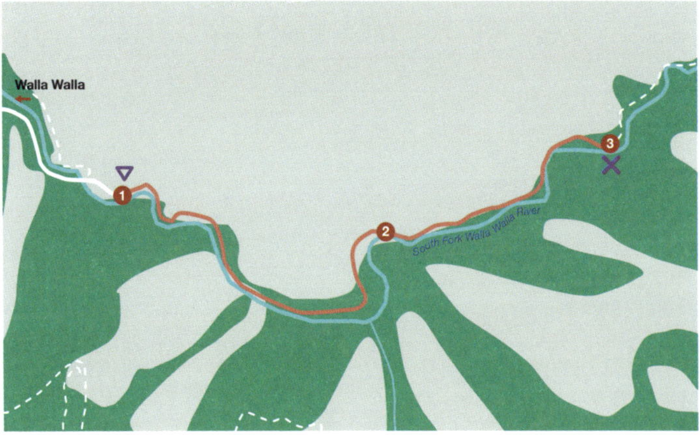

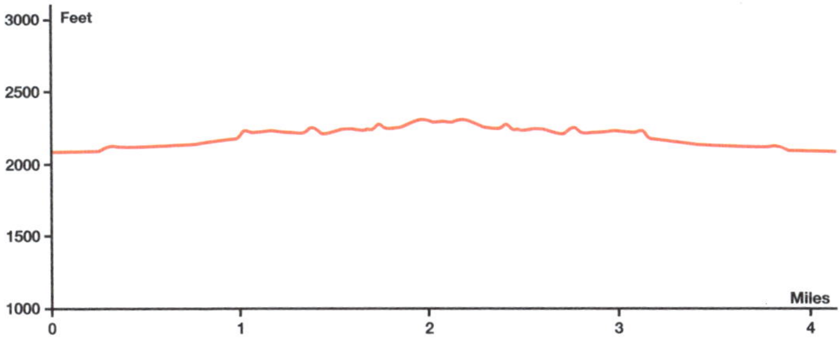

HIKE DESCRIPTION

Hike eastern Oregon and then have a sip on the "meaty" rocks.

Just south of the Oregon–Washington border lies the South Fork Walla Walla trailhead, a popular hiking spot. Our trail begins at Harris Park and follows the South Fork Walla Walla River. With scents of the fresh forest and the sound of the river all around you, you'll trek along a winding river trail flanked by a steep canyon wall on either side. You'll notice a dramatic shift in terrain as the treeless grasslands of Walla Walla suddenly transition to the forested North Fork Umatilla Wilderness and the rugged eastern Oregon mountains. To your left, beyond the looming canyon cliff face, lies Blalock Mountain, named after a certain Doctor Blalock. The doctor's granddaughter recounted in an interview with the *Union-Bulletin* that he was a likable character who garnered a reputation from farmers as being "a damn fool doctor with more money than brains." Regardless, he was loved in the community and made a significant contribution to the area's economic expansion with his massive wheat farming and lumber operations.

The area surrounding Walla Walla and the Blue Mountains has historically had a strong Native American presence. The primary tribes of Walla Walla are the Sahaptin-speaking people (including the famous Nez Perce tribe). The Hudson Bay Company was heavily involved in trading operations throughout the region and the Blue Mountains just south of Walla Walla. You can even visit the cabin of a former French Canadian fur trapper who settled in the area. The rugged eastern Oregon wilderness is sure to surprise visitors not just with its beauty but also with the quality of its wines, including those at the Zerba Cellars vineyard, a mere 20 minutes' drive from the trailhead.

TURN-BY-TURN DIRECTIONS

1. From the trailhead and campground proceed along the North Fork River and Trail.
2. At 1.2 miles, reach a river overlook.
3. At 2.1 miles, reach a bend in the river. Return the way you came.

FIND THE TRAILHEAD

Heading southwest on South Columbia Street in Milton-Freewater, drive 0.7 miles (South Columbia becomes South Main Street). Turn left onto State Highway 11 and proceed for 100 feet before taking a slight right onto South Main Street. Follow South Main Street for 0.1 miles; then turn left on SE 15th Avenue. Proceed for 0.3 miles, continuing onto Walla Walla River Road. Proceed for 4.6 miles on Walla Walla River Road before turning right onto South Fork Walla Walla River Road. Drive another 8.1 miles. The trailhead is at the dead end.

ZERBA CELLARS

While many people associate Walla Walla with Washington wine country, the valley actually extends across the border into Oregon, which has its own Walla Walla winemaking niche. Zerba Cellars is one of Walla Walla's best Oregon wineries. The former owners of a garden nursery, Cecil and Marilyn Zerba craft several great wines that have received accolades in wine competitions across the Pacific Northwest. Wine lovers will enjoy their diverse offerings, including Semillon, Grenache, Cabernet Franc, Viognier, Tempranillo, and even Carmenere. Zerba is located in the Milton-Freewaters "Rocks District," named for the thousands of basalt cobblestones that litter the landscape, which range from small pebbles to softball-sized rocks. But where do they come from? Over thousands of years, the Walla Walla River, which flows from the Blue Mountains, eroded and carried volcanic material downstream into the valley. As the river current slowed, the gravel and basalt cobblestones were deposited, becoming what geologists call an "alluvial fan." The river was eventually redirected elsewhere, leaving the former riverbed an ideal location for present-day winemakers to plant their vineyards. Many claim these rocks lend a distinctive "meaty," "gamey," and "mineral" flavor to the wine, and some even claim that tasting their bottlings is akin to "licking a rock."

Regardless of whether these rocks influence the grapes, the wines of this region are distinct and reflect a sense of place. The international reputation of the Rocks is built on the regional Syrah, which wineries

craft with expressive, distinct, and exciting results. Many wines of Walla Walla are incredibly bold, and Zerba Cellars's are no exception. Driven by rich, powerful fruit, toasty chocolate on the midpalate, and an extensive spicy finish, the Zerba Cellars Rocks Syrah stands out among the wines of the Walla Walla Rocks District.

Syrah: Known as Shiraz in Australia, Syrah is noted for having a distinctive peppery and spicy aroma that pairs wonderfully with a variety of meats. Originating in the south of France, Syrah can be crafted in both cool and warm climates, each of which create distinct but equally interesting expressions of the grape.

LAND MANAGER

Umatilla National Forest
Supervisor's Office
72510 Coyote Road
Pendleton, Oregon 97801
Phone: (541) 278-3716
www.fs.usda.gov

WINERY

Zerba Cellars
85530 OR-11
Milton-Freewater, OR 97862
Phone: (541) 938-9463
www.zerbacellars.com
Distance from trailhead: 14.2 miles

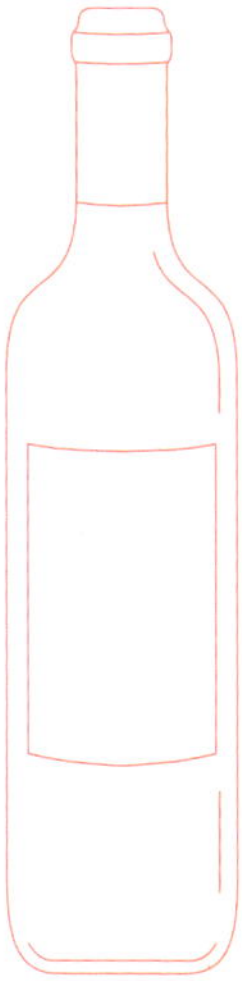

CENTRAL OREGON

MISERY RIDGE AND SUMMIT TRAIL

HIKE OREGON'S ICONIC VOLCANIC CALDERA

STARTING POINT	DESTINATION
CROOKED RIVER DRIVE	MISERY RIDGE/ MONKEY FACE
WINERY	**HIKE TYPE**
FAITH HOPE & CHARITY VINEYARDS	STRENUOUS
DOG FRIENDLY	**SEASON**
YES (LEASH REQUIRED)	YEAR-ROUND
FEES	**DURATION**
$5.00 DAY USE FEE	3 HOURS
MAP REFERENCE	**LENGTH**
POSTED AT TRAILHEAD	6 MILES (LOOP)
HIGHLIGHTS	**ELEVATION GAIN**
THE THREE SISTERS	1,774 FEET

MARQUETTE

ESTATE MARQUETTE

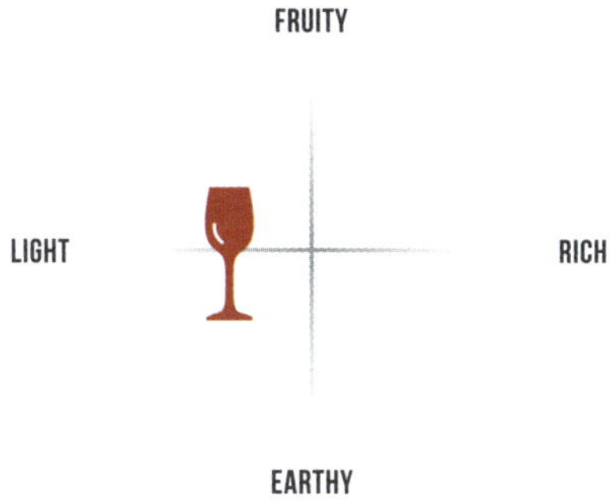

RED,
DRY,
STILL

PEACH,
CITRIC,
FLORAL,
PINEAPPLE,
STONEFRUIT

RED

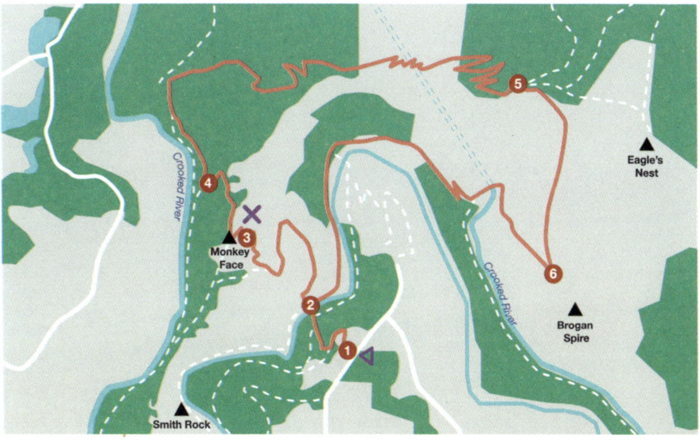

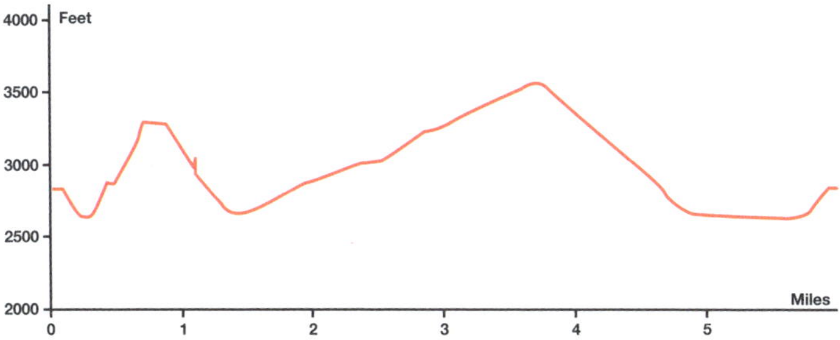

HIKE DESCRIPTION

Hike across an iconic caldera to a famous rock shaped like the face of a monkey. After the hike, sit back and enjoy a tasting at a high-desert wine oasis.

It would be an injustice not to mention the crown jewel of Oregon hiking adventures, Smith Rock. The terrain seems surreal and the surrounding views are sublime—so perfect that the landscape seems like a computer-generated image. This majestic caldera is a raw icon of Oregon's illustrious beauty. Countless visitors have reflected that it looks as though the crags and ravines, the towering pillars, and the bed of the Crooked River, flanked by battlements of rusted red rock, were all fashioned by some colossal ancient titan. Indeed, there is some truth to this: the volcanic titans have worked for millions of years to give hundreds of hikers each year a unique geologic adventure. Sitting on the edge of Oregon's largest caldera, Smith Rock is all that is left of an ancient supervolcano that erupted millions of years ago. The massive formation, known as Crooked River Caldera, is 26 miles long and 17 miles wide. Some geologists believe that this eruption was related to the Yellowstone hotspot. This hike is not to be missed as it is truly an Oregon classic! And speaking of classics, Smith Rock was featured in the John Wayne film *Rooster Cogburn*, the sequel to *True Grit.*

The best time for this hike is early in the morning while the air is still cool. Later in the day, you'll have to face the blistering sun and radiating heat from the rocks. The park does require a day-use permit, which you can purchase either online or at one of the three pay stations in the

park. While our friends who wrote *Beer Hikes Pacific Northwest* already detailed the Misery Ridge Loop, there are several other noteworthy trails in the noble canyon.

Starting at the Rim Rock Trailhead, our path follows the northeastern edge of the caldera ravine. Cross the Crooked River footbridge to the Misery Ridge Trail to begin the ascent with a series of steep switchbacks that head up 600 feet to an upper ridge. At just under a mile, you'll reach the summit and its spectacular views. There's no shortage of photo opportunities during the ascent and at the summit. The path soon descends, giving you the opportunity to view the rock-climbing icon, "Monkey Face." At just over a mile, the path splits left and right along the River Trail. Stay right on the Summit Trail. At roughly 4 miles, the path will ascend a second, rather steep incline that will take you to 3,500 feet! Don't worry, it's downhill from here on out. Join the Wolf River Trail; the last mile is fairly flat, winding along the base of the eastern cliff face and across the Crooked River footbridge toward the Misery Ridge Trailhead.

TURN-BY-TURN DIRECTIONS

1. From the trailhead, follow the Rim Rock Trail and the Chute Path towards the Crooked River Footbridge.
2. At 0.3 miles, cross the Crooked River footbridge. Head straight on the Misery Ridge Trail.
3. At 0.8 miles, arrive at the summit and the viewing area of Monkey Face Rock.
4. At 1.4 miles, stay right and join the Summit Trail.
5. At 3.7 miles, the Summit Trail turns into Burma Road. Continue on Burma Road.
6. At 4.6 miles, stay straight and join the Wolf Tree Trail. Follow the Wolf Tree Trail back to the Crooked River footbridge.

FIND THE TRAILHEAD

From Bend, take US-97 North towards Terrebonne. After 22.8 miles, turn right onto Smith Rock Way and proceed for an additional 0.5 miles; then turn left on Lambert Road and continue for 2.0 miles before turning left onto NE Crooked River Drive. Proceed on NE Crooked River Drive for 0.7 miles to reach the trailhead.

FAITH HOPE & CHARITY VINEYARDS

As you cross the highland desert of Central Oregon, you'll probably think the Gothic white barn with its rainbow arched roof and quaint little pond encircled by lush green vineyards is a desert mirage. In fact, it might be considered a wine oasis. Named after Faith, Hope, and Charity, the original names of the three sister mountains that dominate the highland desert landscape of central Oregon's Bend area, Roger and Cindy Grossmann's establishment offers world-class hospitality. While most conventional wine professionals might discourage wine grape production in a place like Bend, that hasn't stopped the Grossmanns. The winery specializes in cold-hardy hybrid grape varieties like Marquette, La Crescent, Frontenac Gris, and Vignole.

Marquette is the wine of choice at Faith Hope & Charity. This unique hybrid variety is both earthy and fruity; it has a tart backend and a silky texture. While some may snub their nose at hybrids, the winery has nevertheless accrued several notable awards for these unique wines. Faith Hope & Charity also sources fruit from across the Cascades, from both the Willamette and Columbia valleys. Additional offerings of Syrah, Merlot, and Pinot Noir Rosé are available in its tasting room. Faith Hope & Charity offers a world-class guest experience, so expect to be greeted as friends rather than strangers. On weekends, enjoy live music and delicious food, including pizza topped with mushrooms, sausage, pepperoni, garlic chicken, or basil, and seasonal salads and soups. This place offers high-desert wine, top-notch cuisine, and exceptional hospitality.

Marquette: Developed in 2006 by the breeding program at the University of Minnesota, Marquette is a hybrid variety designed to handle the harsh winters in regions like Bend, Oregon. Marquette wines are characterized by dark berry and tobacco flavors, with earthy and spicy undertones.

LAND MANAGER

Oregon Parks and Recreation Department
725 Summer Street NE, Suite C
Salem, OR 97301
Phone: (800) 551-6489
www.oregon.gov

WINERY

Faith Hope & Charity Vineyards
70450 NW Lower Valley Drive
Terrebonne, Oregon 97760
Phone: (541) 526-5075
www.faithhopeandcharityevents.com
Distance from trailhead: 11.5 miles

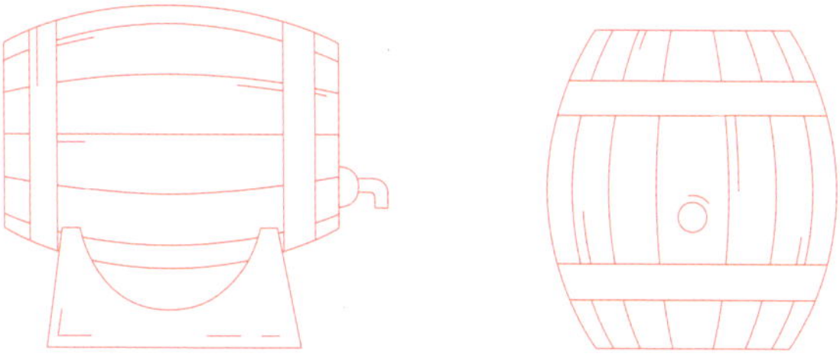

TUMALO FALLS

A HIGHLAND DESERT WATERFALL

STARTING POINT	DESTINATION
SKYLINER SNO-PARK	TUMALO FALLS
WINERY	**HIKE TYPE**
VA PIANO	MODERATE/ STRENUOUS
DOG FRIENDLY	**SEASON**
NO	YEAR-ROUND
FEES	**DURATION**
$5 DAY-USE	1.5 HOURS
MAP REFERENCE	**LENGTH**
POSTED AT TRAILHEAD	6.4 MILES (ROUND-TRIP)
HIGHLIGHTS	**ELEVATION GAIN**
DOWNTOWN MILL DISTRICT	560 FEET

SYRAH

STONEY VINE SYRAH

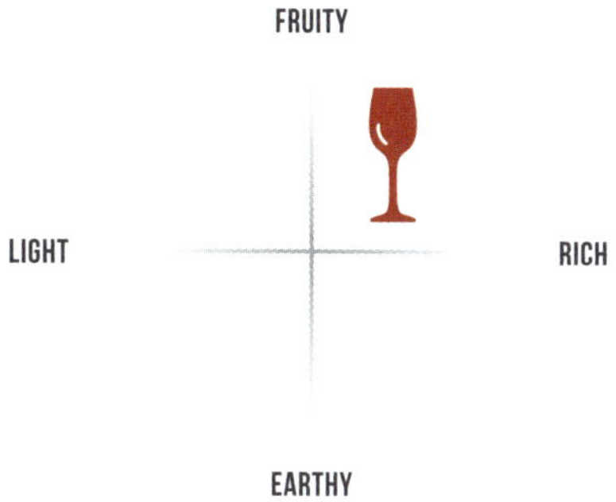

RED,
DRY,
STILL

BLACKBERRY,
DARK OAK,
TIGHT TANNINS

CRIMSON PURPLE

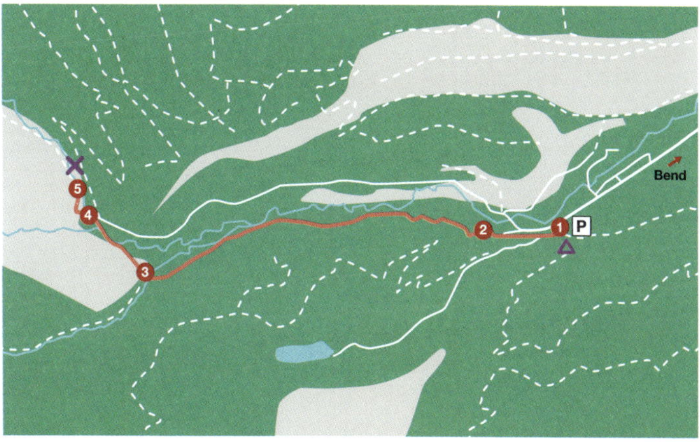

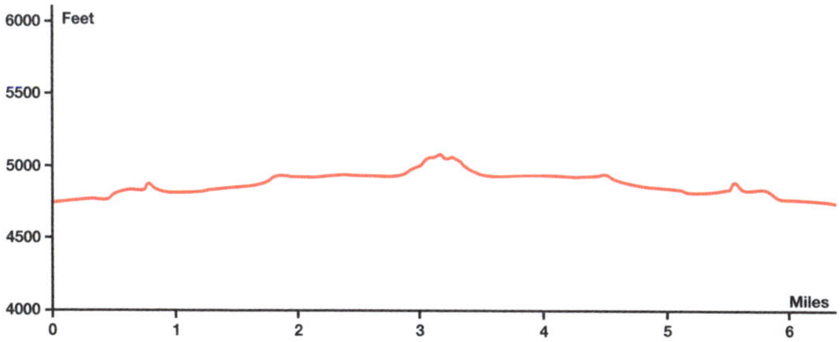

HIKE DESCRIPTION

Hike to one of eastern Oregon's most stunning waterfalls. Then "va piano" (slow down) with a tasting in downtown Bend.

Only ten miles from Bend, you'll find Tumalo Falls, a 97-foot waterfall fed by runoff from the Crook Glacier on Broken Top Mountain. Our trail offers jaw-dropping views of it, and if you extend your hike, you'll also see the Upper Tumalo Falls, Bridge Creek Falls, and Double Falls. Our well-marked trail follows Tumalo Creek and concludes at Tumalo Falls. The trail is easy enough to take kids and dogs on, but you'll still feel like you've hiked to the middle of a vast forest. And in some sense, you will have. Tumalo Creek and Tumalo Creek Falls are the result of a 900-foot-thick ice-age glacier that carved out the canyon, leaving a dramatic series of steep cliffs and crags that are now overgrown with forests.

If you do the hike in spring, you'll be greeted with the thick and refreshing scent of juniper trees and wildflowers. But regardless of what time of year you do it, you'll be able to visit additional waterfalls, depending on how far you want to hike. You can continue hiking two miles past Tumalo Falls along the North Fork Trail #24.4 upstream to Double Falls. This also gives you access to both Upper Tumalo Falls and Bridge Creek Falls before heading back again.

TURN-BY-TURN DIRECTIONS

1. From the trailhead, take the Tumalo Falls Trail.
2. At 0.6 miles, reach the junction with the Tumalo Ridge Trail #25.2. Remain on the Tumalo Falls Trail.
3. At 2.5 miles, reach the junction with the South Fork Trail #25. Stay on the Tumalo Falls Trail.
4. At 3.0 miles, arrive at the parking area and the first Tumalo Falls viewpoint. Continue on the Tumalo Falls Trail.
5. At 3.2 miles, arrive at the falls. Return the way you came.

FIND THE TRAILHEAD

Take Exit 139 from US 97 North. Turn left on SE Reed Market Road and continue for 0.5 miles. At the traffic circle, take the second exit and stay on SW Reed Market Road for another 0.3 miles. At the next traffic circle, stay straight on SW Reed Market Road. Continue for 0.7 miles. At the next traffic circle, take the second exit onto Mt. Washington Drive; follow Mt. Washington Drive for 0.8 miles. At the next traffic circle, stay straight on NW Mt. Washington Drive. After 0.8 miles, at the next traffic circle, take the third exit onto Skyliners Drive. Proceed for 8.8 miles on Skyliners Drive and then take a slight right onto Tumalo Falls Road. After 2.6 miles, turn left into the parking lot marked Skyliner Sno-Park and Trailhead.

VA PIANO

Justin Wylie caught the wine bug while spending his senior year of college in Florence, Italy. "Va Piano," which means "Go Slowly" in Italian, has become more than just a mantra for Justin; it is his winemaking philosophy. Justin focuses on creating gradual improvements to achieve perfection. Va Piano is a Washington winery with Oregon wines: While most of Va Piano's grapes are grown within the borders of Washington State, fruit for Justin's Stony Vine Syrah is grown on the Oregon side of Walla Walla Valley, within the "Rocks District." If you're looking to deviate from the delicate Oregon Pinot Noir, look no further, as this wine displays both hutzpah and richness. It's a bigger wine, with dense fruit, encased with oak and firm tannins. Enjoy the Stony Vine Syrah with a juicy steak or hardy lamb shawarma. The tasting room, located in the Mill District of Bend, offers a relaxed atmosphere and an assortment of beverages other than wine—after all, it wouldn't be Bend, Oregon without a local craft beer! If you're not in the mood for wine or beer, try a craft cider, hard kombucha, or hard seltzer paired with a tasty snack.

LAND MANAGER

Deschutes National Forest
Bend-Fort Rock Ranger District
63095 Deschutes Market Road
Bend, OR 97701
Phone: (541) 383-5300
www.fs.usda.gov

WINERY

Va Piano
425 SW Powerhouse Drive 301
Bend, OR 97702
Phone: (541) 797-6363
www.vapianovineyards.com/bend
Distance from trailhead: 11.3 miles

LAVA RIVER CAVE HIKE

A JOURNEY INTO A LAVA UNDERWORLD

STARTING POINT	DESTINATION
CAVE ENTRANCE	END OF CAVE
WINERY	**HIKE TYPE**
BLEDSOE FAMILY WINERY	EASY
DOG FRIENDLY	**SEASON**
YES (LEASH REQUIRED)	MAY–SEPTEMBER
FEES	**DURATION**
$5 DAY PASS	3 HOURS
MAP REFERENCE	**LENGTH**
POSTED AT TRAILHEAD	2.2 MILES (ROUND-TRIP)
HIGHLIGHTS	**ELEVATION GAIN**
LAVA LANDS VISITOR CENTER	1,774 FEET

SYRAH

STOLEN HORSE SYRAH

FRUITY

LIGHT RICH

EARTHY

RED,
DRY,
STILL

DARK CHERRY,
SPICE,
COCOA,
BLACKBERRY

CRIMSON PURPLE

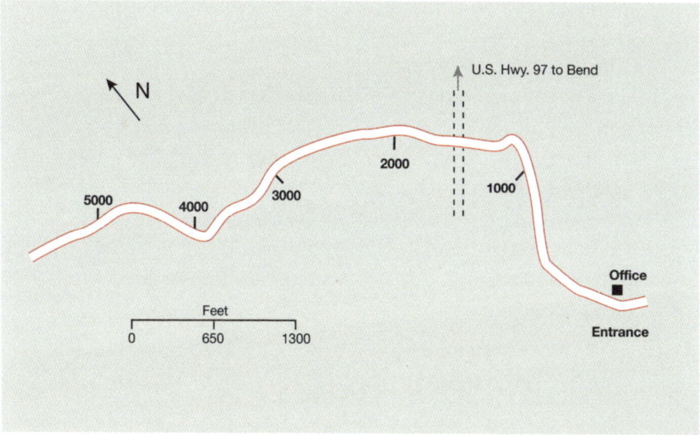

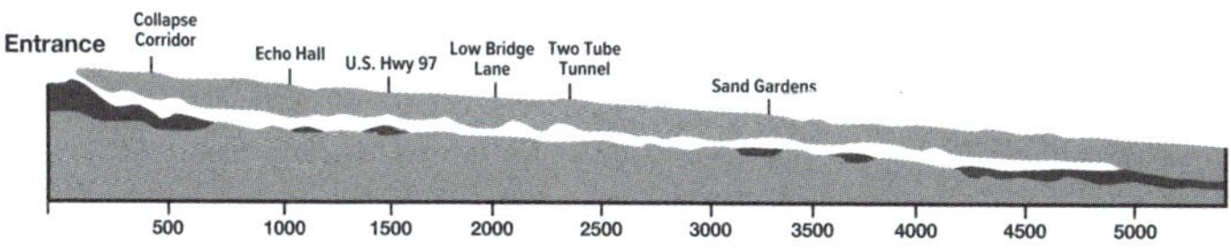

HIKE DESCRIPTION

"Journey to the Center of the Earth" through an ancient lava cave. Then take your wine-tasting game plan to a winery owned by a New England Patriots Hall of Famer.

Lava River Cave is a one of Bend, Oregon's outdoor selling points and is the longest lava tube in the state. It was formed when the surface of a lava river cooled and solidified as the molten lava below drained out. This lava hiking adventure reminds me of Jules Verne's novel, *Journey to the Center of the Earth.*

As you begin your descent down 55 steel steps, the temperature will drop rapidly. Be sure to bring a jacket and flashlight. Even on hot summer days, the temperature can plummet to 42 degrees Fahrenheit (5.5 degrees Celsius). The cave will invoke a sense of mystery with its quiet and its echoing acoustics. The hike will take you to six points of interest, from low ceilings to double tunnels. The cave is a full mile long; when you reach the end, you'll turn around and head back out the way you came.

You'll need a "Timed Reservation Ticket" and a valid recreation pass, which can be purchased on the National Forest Service website. The park also accepts the Northwest Forest Pass, Interagency Passes, Day Pass , and the Newberry National Volcanic Monument Three-Day Pass. The tickets and all park passes can be purchased through the US Forest Service at www.fs.usda.gov. The park is open from May through September. Be sure to check on the opening hours, as they change with the seasons.

TURN-BY-TURN DIRECTIONS

1. From the parking lot, check into the Visitors Center building.
2. Follow the path to the cave entrance.
3. From the cave entrance, descend 55 stairs through Collapse Corridor.
4. Reach Echo Hall and proceed an additional 1500 feet.
5. Continue through Low Bridge Lane for 500 feet. The ceiling drops to 5.5 feet.
6. Enter the Two Tube Tunnel and continue for 500 feet.
7. Reach the Sand Gardens and continue for 700 feet.
8. Reach the end after continuing 1,000 more feet. Return the way you came.

FIND THE TRAILHEAD

From Bend, take Highway 97 South. Exit right onto Crawford Road/NF-9702 and follow it for 0.1 miles. Turn left onto Cottonwood Road and continue for 1.2 miles. Turn right into the parking lot marked "Lava River Cave."

BLEDSOE FAMILY WINERY

If you think American football and wine don't pair well, think again. Former Patriots quarterback and Walla Walla (Washington State) native Drew Bledsoe went from scoring touchdowns (271 of them!) in the NFL to scoring touchdowns with his wines. He founded Bledsoe Family Winery shortly after retiring from the game and sought to establish himself as a wine producer in the critically acclaimed wine region of Walla Walla. Working with winemaker Josh McDaniels—a fellow Walla Walla native and winemaking veteran of Leonetti Cellars—Drew focused on crafting a variety of wines from Cabernet Sauvignon and Syrah grapes. Most recently, he has added a Pinot Noir from the Willamette Valley. While the primary estate is located in Walla Walla, Bledsoe sources much of his fruit from Oregon. Like Batman and Robin, Drew and Josh are a winning team. They produce several noteworthy wines that will excite your tastebuds. Bledsoe Family Winery is the perfect place to sit back and taste wine after a hike through a lava cave in eastern Oregon.

LAND MANAGER

Deschutes National Forest
Lava Lands Visitor Center
58201 South Highway 97
Bend, OR 97707
Phone: (541) 593-2421
www.fs.usda.gov

WINERY

Bledsoe Family Winery
550 SW Industrial Way, Suite 198
Bend, OR 97702
Phone: (541) 797-6502
www.bledsoefamilywinery.com
Distance from trailhead: 13.8 miles

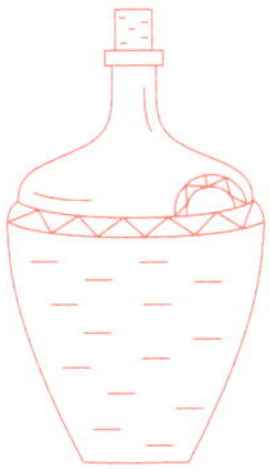

DEDICATION AND ACKNOWLEDGEMENTS

Often, our lives change unexpectedly and at a moment's notice. That's what happened to me with this book. It was late one January night when I received a message from Richard Harvell, head of Helvetiq's USA publishing department. "We need an author for a book," he said. "Would you be interested in writing it?" It didn't seem real!

Thus was *Wine Hikes Oregon* born. The timing was impeccable. I was just about to graduate from college. My diploma was still warm off the press when I packed my last belongings into a small Lexus and set off to Oregon. It was comical, really. I had hardly unpacked before I found myself immersed in the writing process, hiking, discovering new wines and wineries, and experiencing the splendor of Oregon's spectacular mountain views, rolling countryside, and roaring waterfalls.

Wine Hikes Oregon is dedicated to my favorite plot twist: Hannah, the love of my life, best friend, the girl at the Italian Café. You are the greatest source of unwavering love, support, and encouragement. As Beatrice guided Dante, you have been beside me, editing my first blog, challenging me, and helping grow me into a better man.

And to my mother, Danielle. From beginning to end, late nights and early mornings, you proofread every page of this book. I truly would not have been able to complete this book without your love, help, and support.

I would like to thank Ashley Curtis, my copyeditor. You are nothing short of extraordinary at your craft. I thank you for your hard work, your patience with a first-time author, and the much appreciated positive and constructive criticism that transformed me into a better writer. This book would be nothing without you. It was both an honor and a privilege to work with you.

Many thanks to Richard Harvell. Little did I know that your surprise LinkedIn message at 12:15 a.m. one winter night would result in this amazing journey. Thank you, Richard. At the tender age of five years old, I dreamed of writing a book. You helped that dream come true.

I'd also like to thank Daniel Malak, our graphic designer extraordinaire. You took the ideas that were in my head and laid them out on paper. Thank you for the hard work and your immense patience.

Thanks also to Hadi Barkat, CEO of Helvetiq for the phenomenal opportunity to write this book.

Thank you, Grant *DM* and our favorite mountain man, James. Your continuous comic relief and stupendously witty humor added a very entertaining element to the hiking process. If there were a book about comedy and hiking, you'd be the authors.

Thanks also to Wade Smith. Those long hours in the cellar with you were well spent. Your patience and encouragement taught me never to give up. Much of the knowledge about wine you gave me has found its way into this book.

And to Stephen and Gloria Reustle, my second father and mother. You both have been ceaseless in your love, encouragement, and amazing support. It was you, Stephen who took me under your wing and began teaching me about wine. You have always believed in me and continue to do so. If we had never met, this book would not exist.

Many thanks to Rick and Jeanette Bailor. You two were wonderful to travel with. Thank you for our many enjoyable afternoons hunting for wineries.

Many thanks to Greg Jones, Dan Marca, Cindy Grossmann, Franco and Sandy Marchesi, Dionne Irvine, Steven Sinkler, and Carole Astley. It was a joy working with you all to create great content for this book.

Much gratitude to all the tasting-room staff and associates at each of the wineries. To the staff of Irvine and Roberts, many thanks and sorry if I accidentally terrified you all! You were terrific.

And finally, to everyone involved whom I haven't mentioned by name. There were so many of you—people who, both directly and indirectly, played a role in the creation of *Wine Hiking Oregon.*

BEER HIKING
PACIFIC NORTHWEST
THE TASTIEST WAY TO DISCOVER
WASHINGTON, OREGON, AND BRITISH COLUMBIA
NEW AND UPDATED EDITION
RACHEL WOOD
BRANDON FRALIC
45 MIN.
52 CRAFT BREWERIES
HANDPICKED HIKES

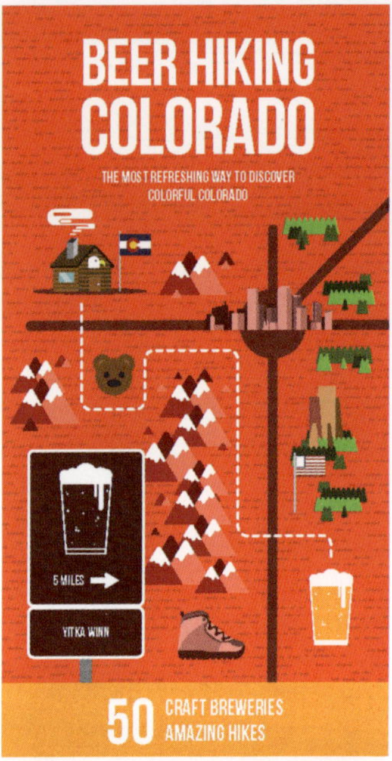
BEER HIKING
COLORADO
THE MOST REFRESHING WAY TO DISCOVER
COLORFUL COLORADO
5 MILES
YITKA WINN
50 CRAFT BREWERIES
AMAZING HIKES

RANDOS BIÈRE
AU QUÉBEC
LA FAÇON LA PLUS RAFRAÎCHISSANTE DE VOIR LE QUÉBEC
12 KM
BIANCA POMERLEAU

BEER HIKING
NEW ENGLAND
THE TASTIEST WAY TO DISCOVER MAINE,
NEW HAMPSHIRE, VERMONT, MASSACHUSETTS,
CONNECTICUT AND RHODE ISLAND
CAREY KISH
20 MIN.
50 CRAFT BREWERIES
HANDPICKED HIKES

Coming soon:

BEER HIKING NEW YORK

BEER HIKING SOUTHERN CALIFORNIA

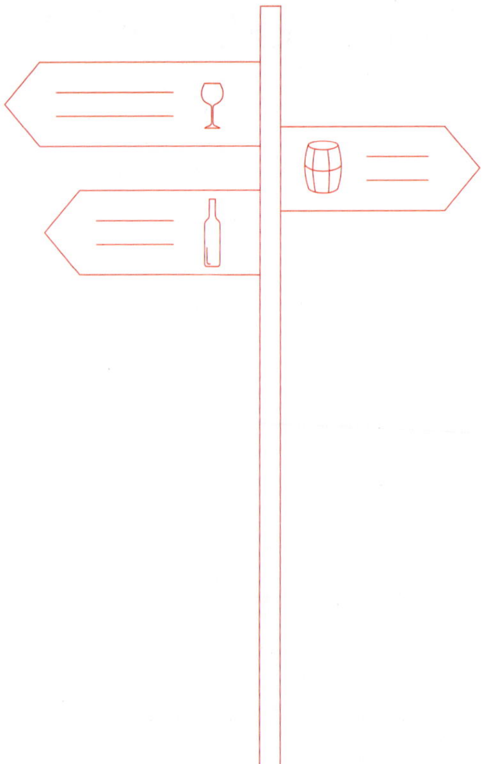